Bridges of Promise

REVISED EDITION

D1402520

Bridges of Promise
Taking Steps to Follow Jesus

REVISED EDITION

Franklin W. Nelson

Judson Press
Valley Forge

Bridges of Promise: Taking Steps to Follow Jesus, Revised Edition
© 2001 by Judson Press, Valley Forge, PA 19482–0851

Bible quotations in this volume are from Today's English Version, Second Edition © 1992 by American Bible Society. Used by permission.

Interior illustrations by Gwendolyn Wong

Library of Congress Cataloging-in-Publication Data

Nelson, Franklin W.
    Bridges of promise : taking steps to follow Jesus / Franklin W. Nelson.—Rev. ed.
        p. cm.
    ISBN 0–8170–1359–8 (pbk : alk. paper)
    1. Christian education of children. 2. Christian education—Activity programs. 3. Baptists—Education.
I. Title.

BV1475.2.N45 2001
268'.432—dc21   00–063870

Printed in the U.S.A.

07 06 05 04

10 9 8 7 6 5 4 3 2

WHAT'S IN THIS BOOK?

(To complete the chapter titles of this book, fill in each blank with your own name.)

FROM THE WRITER

WHAT IS A PROMISE?

Long ago I made a promise to Judson Press that I would write a book. The title for the book was *Bridges of Promise*. It was a lot of work, and I doubt I would ever have completed the project if I had not made a promise to do it. But I said I would and I did, largely because of the encouragement I received from many. The first edition was published in 1990.

That's why promises are so important! If we keep our promises, there is the possibility that something new will be created.

God's promise to love us is like that. In fact, the Bible is a book about God's promises to us, but that's not all. It's also a book about the promises we need to make to God. We are all invited to love God with all of our heart, mind, soul and strength.

Will you believe in Jesus Christ and promise to live your life as one of his disciples and followers? If you say yes to that invitation and really mean it, it will become the most important promise you'll ever make, because it will shape your life and give you the promise of new life in Christ.

And so I want to promise you that if you choose Jesus Christ as your guide and companion throughout life, you will experience a wonderful adventure full of many challenges and surprises. And you will know that God loves you—forever. It's a promise.

WHAT IS THE PURPOSE OF A BRIDGE?

Bridges help us travel over hard-to-cross places. They help us get from one side to the other. The journey from birth to death is like a long bridge. How do we cross the bridge of life successfully? How do we know that we are going in the direction God wants us to go? How can we be sure that we are on our way to live forever with God?

In John 14:6, Jesus says, "I am the way." In other words, Jesus is like a bridge. He's the one who shows us how to live and how to discover God. The word disciple means "student" or "learner." That's what we are in our relationship with Jesus Christ—students! Jesus wants to teach us how to live our lives successfully.

One of the new features of this revised study is that you will be asked to read the story of Jesus in the book of Mark. Why is that important? The more we know about Jesus, the more we will be amazed by him, grow to love him, and desire to make him the most important person in our lives.

As one who has been crossing life's bridge for a long time, I offer you the best advice I can: follow Jesus. Learn about him, discover that he loves you, and live your life's journey—all of it—as one of his disciples. If that's what you decide to do, you won't be sorry. It's a promise!

I WISH TO THANK ...

Jesus Christ, my personal Lord and Savior,
for being the most influential person of my life.

Alvin and Evelyn Nelson, my parents,
who taught me the importance of faith in Jesus Christ.

Rosemary, my wife, who teaches me daily by her example
the meaning of living the Christian life.

Angela Nelson, my daughter, who inspired me to write
the first edition of *Bridges of Promise*,
and has now dedicated her life to the mission of Christ in this world.

Paul Nelson, my older son,
the first to go through *Bridges of Promise* with his pastor/dad.

Joel Nelson, my younger son, who experienced *Bridges of Promise*
shortly after it was first published.
Joel became a follower of Jesus Christ
and was baptized as a member of the church.

The people and children of Woodbury Baptist Church, my home church,
for blessing me with their emotional and prayerful support
in this creative work beyond the local church setting.

The American Baptist Churches USA,
the denomination of my birth and my wider church family,
for keeping my Baptist roots alive and giving us
all the people of Judson Press who creatively serve
Christ and our local churches.

INTRODUCTION

A Message for Older Children and Younger Youth

WELCOME!

During this study you're invited to use your imagination as you become a part of a class taking place at First Baptist Church. You will meet Pastors David and Maria, the new pastors of First Baptist, and be invited to their apartment to enjoy pizza and the joy of learning more about what it means to follow Jesus. You will also be invited to become a part of their first "pastor's class" with some of the children from First. The resource they have chosen to use for the study is *Bridges of Promise*. You will meet the five children who have decided to be a part of the class—Angela, Tyrel, Daniel, Joy, and Esteban.

Each of the eight chapters begins with a story. During each story you will be invited to do the same activities, read the same Scriptures, and discuss the same questions as the class. When you see the activity icon, stop and take time to do the activity. When you see the discussion icon, stop to discuss the topic, and so on.

In addition to the weekly stories and activities, you will be expected to complete the daily assignments:

1. First, you will read the "Scripture for Today" in the Bible and write responses to the sentence completion exercise that follows.
2. Next, you'll be asked to look up the dictionary definition for one of the BIG WORDS of the Christian faith and then think about what the word means to you.
3. Finally, you'll be invited to write your own "Prayer for the Day."

If you can, choose a regular time and place each day for completing the assignment. Promise yourself that you will finish all the assignments in time for each week's class. It's easier if you make a promise!

A MESSAGE FOR PARENTS, PASTORS, AND ADULT LEADERS

This resource can be used one-on-one or as a guide to follow with a group of older children and/or younger youth. One of the unique features of the book is that it provides an easy-to-follow guide for Christian parents who want to be involved in the faith and teaching of their own children.

You'll find that the "leader's guide" has been integrated into the weekly story. So as the text describes Pastors David and Maria and the children doing an activity, take time to complete the same activity. Use the icons contained in the material as guides.

Each week you will need to plan ahead for the next session. Read the story carefully. Gather the materials you will need (scissors, markers, pencils, and so on) for the activities. Review the activity sheets in the back of the book. (Important note: It is best not to skip any of the activities. Each one is an integral part of the study.) Also, remember that food helps to create a positive learning environment. Plan to have a snack along with the study.

A MESSAGE TO PARENTS WHO WANT TO DISCIPLE/TEACH THEIR OWN CHILDREN AT HOME

This study outline provides a user-friendly way for parents or grandparents to be actively involved in discipling their own children or grandchildren. The Christian home needs to be a place where faith is taught, lived, and caught by children and youth. This resource gives parents who want to be directly involved the tool they need for discipling their children in their own home.

If you are a parent who has chosen to mentor your own child, invite your pastor to meet with you and your child (or with a group of interested parents and children) to guide you through Session One and to launch the study and clarify expectations. Following Session One, your child will be expected to complete each daily assignment before continuing with Session Two. Be available to help your child with the daily assignments; in some cases, it is appropriate for the parent and child to work side-by-side in completing the assignments. Then, you and your child will meet in your home for Session Two to review the daily assignments, read the story together and complete all of the activities and discussions that are a part of the chapter story.

When your child has completed the material for chapters 1 through 5, invite your pastor to become involved once again for the class on baptism and Communion in chapter 6. This will give your pastor the opportunity to review the work your child has done, help to assess your child's readiness for baptism, and answer any questions you or your child may have about baptism and Communion.

If this material is used as a traditional "pastor's class," I recommend that parents be involved, especially during the first class, so that they can understand the value of the daily assignments and learn how to be supportive of their children's experiences throughout the *Bridges of Promise* study.

A WORD TO ADULTS ABOUT THE SPIRITUAL READINESS OF CHILDREN

This study has been written with older children (ten- to twelve-year-olds) in mind, many of whom are at an age when they read, think abstractly, and are ready to make life-long decisions. But this material will work well, also, with thirteen- to fifteen-year-olds and/or eight- to nine-year-olds depending on the readiness of the individual child.

In physical, emotional, mental, and spiritual development, each child develops at his/her own unique pace. It is important that adults (in their eagerness to help their children become disciples) resist the temptation to rush or push a child toward a commitment to Jesus Christ. Pray for wisdom to watch for signs of resistance. Be very patient with your child. Remember, too, that some fifteen-year-olds may not be ready while some eight-year-olds may be very ready. Prayerfully, let the Holy Spirit of wisdom and love guide you in understanding the spiritual readiness of each child/youth.

PRAYER IS IMPORTANT

Prayer is a powerful resource. Rely on God to be at work in the life of the children and youth who are in the process of becoming disciples of Jesus Christ. Pray, not only for the child or children in your care, but for children everywhere, that they might discover faith in Christ and make the promise to follow Jesus as their personal Lord and Savior.

CHAPTER 1

GOD CREATED

_____

(Write your name here.)

AS A "MOUNTAIN OF PROMISE"

DAY 1: WEEK 1  ● MON ● TUE ● WED ● THU ● FRI ● SAT ● SUN (Check One)

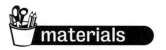 materials

Copies of _Bridges of Promise_, Bibles, scissors, tape, and colored markers. Review Activity #1, "Getting Acquainted," and Activity #2, "Mountain of Promise."

THE STORY: NEW BEGINNINGS

Pastors Maria and David were new to First Baptist. One of the first things they decided to do after arriving at the church was to send an invitation to the older children of First, especially those who had not yet made a public commitment to Jesus Christ and been baptized, to come to their home for the first meeting of _Bridges of Promise_. The invitation said, "The purpose of this class is to explore the meaning of being a follower of Jesus Christ and a member of the church." In the invitation, Pastor David promised homemade, hand-tossed pepperoni pizza. That was his specialty because Pastor David had worked his way through seminary tossing pizzas.

It sounded good to Angela, Esteban, Joy, Tyrel, and Daniel, so they said they would come. The group met at Pastor Maria and David's new apartment. After they were done eating, the children helped with clean-up. Everyone agreed that Pastor David's was the best pizza they had ever tasted.

Pastor Maria moved to the computer desk. "Let's log on to the Internet and see if we can find the American Baptist website." The children were curious as Maria searched for www.abc-usa.org, the website for American Baptist Churches USA. When she clicked on "Who We Are," an icon for *Bridges of Promise* appeared. The children crowded closer to see her click again, and "From the Writer" appeared on the screen.

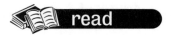 **read**

If you have Internet access, log on at www.abc-usa.org and follow the pathway described above to *Bridges of Promise*. Take time now to read "From the Writer," either on the web page or from the *Bridges of Promise* book on page vi.

discussion

After reading "From the Writer," discuss:
- What is a promise?
- Why are promises so important?
- Describe a promise you have made.
- Has anyone ever broken a promise to you? What was it like?

As they explored the website further, the children were excited to discover that all those who complete the *Bridges of Promise* study are invited to register their name, state, and country. The children were amazed to find that there are thousands of children around the world who have completed *Bridges of Promise*.

Pastor David continued, "Let's open our books to page v, 'What's in This Book?' Notice that the chapter titles are incomplete, so write your first name in each of the titles."

activity

As the children wrote their names, Pastor David read each of the titles to give the students a preview of the topics they will be exploring during the eight-week study.

Pastor Maria continued, "Now open your books to chapter 1 and write your name in the title for chapter 1, 'God Created _____ as a Mountain of Promise.'"

"During the next few weeks we'll be exploring what it means to be a terrific disciple of Jesus Christ," Pastor Maria explained. "But first, let's get better acquainted with one another. Find Activity #1, 'Getting Acquainted,' on page 141 and take time now to fill it in."

 activity

When everyone had finished writing, the children and pastors each took time to tell the group about themselves.

Then Pastor Maria began to read the opening paragraphs in the *Bridges of Promise* book:

> Did you know that God thinks you're terrific!
> How do we know?
> God has given you this wonderful world to enjoy, and God has given you
> a *body* in which you can grow,
> a *heart* with which you can feel and you can love,
> a *mind* with which you can think and know and choose,
> and a *soul* that will live forever.
>
> You are loved.
> You are an amazing gift.
> You are a promise of God.
>
> But many of us sometimes wonder…
> How do I discover the "terrific" in me?
> How do I make the most of my life?
> How can I be the best that I can be?
> Where is God?
> Who is God?
> Does God know me?
> Does God really think that I'm terrific?

"These are just some of the questions you and I might have about God and our lives," Pastor Maria said. "What are some other questions you have?"

discussion

"I can tell that you guys are going to keep David and me on our toes in the coming weeks," Pastor Maria concluded with a laugh as the discussion wound down.

Next, Pastor David handed the children scissors, clear tape, and a box of colored markers. "We're going to create 'Mountains of Promise' to help us talk about just how special we are. Turn to the Activity Section at the back of your books and remove Activity #2, 'Mountain of Promise,' on page 143."

activity

Pastor David continued, "Use your scissors and cut on the bold lines. As you're doing that, listen carefully to these two Scripture passages. The first is from Deuteronomy 6:4–5."

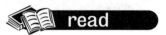
read

Pastor David read the verses for the group. "The Old Testament teaches that we're to love God with all of our heart, soul, and strength. Now listen as Maria reads what Jesus had to say about loving God in the New Testament, Mark 12:28–31."

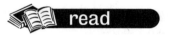
read

Pastor Maria read the passage as the children completed their cutting project. Pastor David continued, "The Bible teaches that one way to love God is with our bodies. Pick a colored marker and write the word body on one of the triangles of your Mountain of Promise."

activity

As the children began writing, Pastor David continued. "One of the very special gifts God has given each of us is a physical self. Without our bodies we would not be able to love God. What's one way we can show that we love God with our body?"

discussion

Esteban, who loved to play soccer said, "Regular exercise is one way we take care of our bodies." Joy, who pitched on a softball team, added, "I think eating well is an important part of taking care of ourselves, not just eating junk food all the time." And Pastor David added, "And not just pizza all the time, either. That's why we added the salad and carrot sticks. We need to eat well-balanced diets."

Pastor Maria smiled in agreement and added, "It's important for those of us who are interested in learning more about Jesus to remember that he gave his body on the cross to show that he loved us. If he did that for us, we need to be willing to give our physical lives in serving and helping others and showing them that we love them."

Pastor Maria continued, "Another word that Jesus used to describe the way we can love God is the word mind. Now take a different color and write the word mind on another side of your Mountain of Promise."

activity

"What are some of the ways we can use our minds to show that we love God?" Pastor David asked.

discussion

Daniel said, "I know that school is important, but sometimes I have a hard time getting good grades. Still, I know that school is important in helping my mind grow." Angela added, "And if we don't go to school, we won't be learning all the things we need to know in order to be all that God wants us to be." Tyrel said, "It's not just school! I think it's important to come to classes like this and learn about the Bible, too."

"Excellent ideas," Pastor David said. "You're terrific! Now on to the next word. Pick a new color and write the word heart."

activity

The class wrote the word as Pastor Maria said, "Sometimes the heart is used to describe the feeling center of a person. Have you ever heard that someone had a 'broken heart'?"

discussion

Pastor David said, "I think I know what that means, because when I was ten, my parents divorced. For a long time I was angry and broken-hearted about it. It still hurts just to mention it."

"I can understand that," Tyrel said, "because my parents divorced two years ago. It's really been hard!"

"God cares about you, Tyrel and David," Pastor Maria said. "God cares about all of us and doesn't want our hearts to be broken, but when they are, God is there to restore and renew our hearts in Jesus Christ. In fact, sometimes we talk about giving our whole heart to something or to someone. What do you think it means to give your heart to something or somebody?"

Esteban said, "I think it's giving it everything you've got! Like when I play soccer, I play with my whole heart!"

"Good example, Esteban," Pastor David said. "When we give our hearts to Jesus, it means we want to live for him and give him everything we've got! We try to love him with all of our hearts. When I was a senior in high school, a friend of mine invited me to his youth group. It was during one of our youth meetings that I decided to promise my life to Jesus Christ. It's made all the difference in the world for me—best thing I ever did!"

Pastor Maria said, "It was a little different for me. I grew up in a church. I was a young child when I first learned how important it was to give my heart and life to Jesus. I was maybe five years old when I first knew that I loved Jesus, and I was twelve when I promised to live my life for him. That's when I decided to be baptized. I agree with

David. It's the best choice I've ever made."

She smiled and said, "David's my second-best choice!"

The group laughed and Pastor David gave an embarrassed smile. The children were starting to enjoy knowing these two who had come as their new pastors. And they could tell there was something special about them.

Pastor David said, "Maria and I have been married for almost two years, and I think that the promise we made to each other in marriage is a lot like the one we make to Jesus Christ. It can't be a half-hearted thing, or just for a few weeks or years. The promise I made to Maria was for a lifetime, and it's the same with Jesus. That's what makes it such an important decision!"

The class was intent on what he was saying and eager to learn more about this promise.

"We're going to run out of time if we don't move on," Pastor Maria said. "There's one more word that describes the way we are to love God. Do you know what Jesus says the fourth word is?"

The class had forgotten, so Pastor Maria read the verse again, "'Love the Lord your God with all your heart, with all your soul, with all your mind, and with all your strength.' So, what's the fourth word?"

"Soul!"

"Pick another color and write the word soul on the fourth side of your mountain."

 activity

As they wrote the word, Pastor David asked, "What do you think the soul is? Do you think you have a soul?"

discussion

The children looked confused by the question, and so Pastor David added, "The soul is maybe the hardest part of us to describe and understand, but let me try. It's like the core of who we really are. We sometimes call the soul our spirit, but whatever it is, it's the part of us that, when our bodies die, lives on forever. And I believe that when we give our heart, soul, mind and body to Jesus Christ, our soul lives forever with God in heaven."

There was a hush in the room as the class pondered this mystery, especially Angela. It had been only a year since her father had died in a terrible car accident, and at the time she remembered thinking a lot about the soul. In fact, when she saw her father's body lying in the casket, she knew that it was only his body and that his spirit and soul were somewhere else. Angela had found comfort in believing the promise that her father's soul was with God forever.

"And so God has given us these incredible, awesome gifts—our bodies, minds, hearts, and souls," Pastor David said. "That's why we're all so terrific! But now it's time to put it all together and complete the final construction of our Mountains of Promise.

Fold the edges on the dotted lines, and then tape the tab on the inside to form the four-sided mountain."

 activity

The class members worked to construct their mountains while Pastor Maria asked, "Have any of you ever been to the mountains?" Several in the group had gone on trips to see the mountains. Esteban said he used to live near the mountains in Guatemala.

"Why do you think our lives—body, mind, heart, and soul—are like Mountains of Promise?" Pastor Maria asked.

 discussion

Tyrel said, "A mountain is created by God, and so are we."

Daniel added, "And a mountain is huge. We may not be all that huge, but in God's eyes, every person has a lot of potential."

Then Esteban added, "Whenever I went to the mountains in Guatemala, I always felt close to God. There's something about the bigness of the mountains that helps you realize just how big and awesome God, our Creator, is."

"And there's something about every person," Pastor Maria added. "In fact, each one of us in this room is awesome. We are very special in God's eyes."

Pastor David added, "My favorite person to talk about is Jesus. Did you know that he was a lot like a Mountain of Promise, and he gave his body, mind, heart, and soul to God. If we're to be his followers, it's very important that we learn all we can about him. During the next several weeks, you'll be expected to read the Gospel of Mark, a few verses each day, because it tells the story of Jesus. By the end of our study, you will have read the whole Gospel of Mark! Let's take a look at our verses for today in Mark 1:1–20."

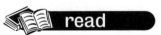 read

The children took turns reading the verses and then filled in the sentence completion blanks before their discussion.

 activity

Scripture for Today: Read Mark 1:1–20

In today's reading I learned that Jesus _____

_____

_____

Jesus was baptized in what river? _____

_____

I think he wanted to be baptized because _____

_____

_____

John preached that we are to "Turn away from our sins and be baptized." For me to "turn away from my sins" means that I am willing to _____

_____

_____

discussion

After they had discussed the Bible verses, Pastor Maria said, "In addition to reading a part of the Bible each day, you'll also have a chance to think about some of the BIG WORDS of our faith. Right now it's time to introduce the BIG WORD for today. Drum roll, please!" Pastor David started pounding the coffee table with his hands.

Pastor Maria announced, "The BIG WORD is FREEDOM. It's one of the most important words to describe a Baptist. Baptists believe that we all have the freedom to decide whether or not we want to believe in Jesus and follow him. Nobody can decide for you. I can't. Your parents can't. You're the only person in the whole world who can decide if you want to be a follower of Jesus Christ."

Pastor David continued, "And it's our hope and prayer that during the weeks ahead each of you will want to make that choice. If you do decide to be a disciple of Jesus, I guarantee you that it will be the most important promise you'll ever make! Right now, let's look up the word *freedom* in the dictionary."

As Pastor David read the definition from Webster, the children wrote it in their books under the word FREEDOM.

activity

The Big Word: FREEDOM

Dictionary definition: _____

_____

_____

I feel "free" when _____

_____

To say I'm free to do or not do something means that I _____

_____

_____

_____

This is what John 8:36 says about freedom: _____

_____

_____

_____

discussion

After their discussion on FREEDOM, Pastor Maria said, "The third part of each of the daily activities is to write a prayer. Prayer is such an important part of our relationship with God. David and I think it's important for you to develop the habit of praying every day. Take some time now to write a prayer in today's assignment."

activity

My Prayer for Today

Dear God, thank you that you have given me the freedom to choose. When I am being faced with a choice, I pray that you will help me to _____

_____

_____

I'm sorry for the times when I choose to _____

_____

_____

As I begin Bridges of Promise, *help me to* _____

_____

_____

Amen.

When the members of the group had completed their prayers, Pastor Maria said, "It's important that you keep up with the daily assignments. If you miss a day, that's okay, but try to make it up the next day."

Pastor David invited the class members to look through the daily assignments for the first week, and the children marked the days of the week for each assignment. It was like setting a goal to complete the assignment for that day.

When the class period was over, Pastor Maria led with this prayer: "Dear God, thank you that you have created us with our bodies, minds, hearts, and souls. Thank you for the freedom to choose for ourselves. Help us to choose to live our lives for you. We want to learn to be your followers. And thank you for my friends and the great time we've had together. Amen."

DAY 2: WEEK 1   ● MON ● TUE ● WED ● THU ● FRI ● SAT ● SUN   (Check One)

Scripture for Today: Read Mark 1:21–39

In today's reading, Jesus *(did what?)* _____

_____

_____

I think Jesus wanted to heal people because _____

_____

_____

Maybe Jesus needed to go to a lonely place to pray because he _____

_____

_____

The Big Word: HEART

Dictionary definition: _____

_____

_____

To do something with "all my heart" means that I _____

_____

_____

To let Jesus "come into my heart" means that I'm willing to _____

_____

_____

_____

To love Jesus with "all of my heart" means that I _____

_____

_____

_____

_____

Ephesians 3:17 says that if we have faith in Christ, he makes his home in our lives (hearts). On the scale below, where is Christ in relationship to your life/heart?

◎——•——•——•——•——•——•——•——•——•——•——◎
Far   1   2   3   4   5   6   7   8   9   10   Very
away   near
from me   (circle one)   to me

Explain: _____

_____

_____

_____

_____

_____

_____

My Prayer for Today

Dear God, thank you that Jesus loved me with all of his heart and gave his life for me. I want you to become more and more a part of my heart and life, so teach me how to

_____

_____

_____

And thank you for the people who love me, including _____

_____

_____

_____

Amen.

DAY 3: WEEK 1 ● MON ● TUE ● WED ● THU ● FRI ● SAT ● SUN (Check One)

Scripture for Today: Read Mark 1:40–2:12

If Jesus healed me of a disease, I think I'd feel _____
_____
_____
_____

Jesus had authority to forgive sins. I think his authority came from _____
_____
_____
_____

I need to ask Jesus to forgive me for the sin of _____
_____
_____
_____

The Big Word: MIND

Dictionary definition: _____
_____
_____
_____

My mind is most alert and alive when I _____
_____
_____
_____

Read Philippians 4:7. One way I can keep my heart and mind "safe in union with Christ Jesus" is to _____
_____
_____
_____
_____
_____

Read Philippians 4:8. Then list some of the things our minds need to be full of: _____
_____
_____
_____
_____

My Prayer for Today

Dear God, thank you that you have given me the gift of my mind, so that I can think and choose. Keep my thoughts pure and good.

Forgive me when I think negative things about _____
_____
_____
_____

Instead help me to think good things about _____
_____
_____
_____

I promise you that I will try to use my mind in positive and good ways as I _____
_____
_____
_____

Amen.

DAY 4: WEEK 1 ● MON ● TUE ● WED ● THU ● FRI ● SAT ● SUN (Check One)

Scripture for Today: Read Mark 2:13–22

In today's reading Jesus *(did what?)* _____
_____
_____
_____

If Jesus said to me, "Follow me!" this is what I'd say to Jesus _____
_____
_____
_____
_____

The Big Word: BODY

Dictionary definition: _____
_____
_____
_____

My body is a wonderful gift to me. Some of the physical features of my body that I like
are _____
_____
_____
_____

Some of the things I wish I could change about my body are _____
_____
_____
_____

I take care of my body whenever I _____
_____
_____
_____

I don't take care of my body when I _____
_____
_____
_____

Read 1 Corinthians 3:16. When I read that our bodies are like temples where the Spirit
of God lives, it makes me feel _____
_____
_____
_____

My Prayer for Today

Dear God, thank you for giving me my body. Forgive me for the times when I don't take care of my body by _____
_____
_____
_____

And thank you, dear God, that your Spirit is able to live in my body. Help me to understand why _____
_____
_____
_____

I promise you that I will try to take care of my body always by _____
_____
_____
_____
_____
_____

Amen.

DAY 5: WEEK 1 ⬤ MON ⬤ TUE ⬤ WED ⬤ THU ⬤ FRI ⬤ SAT ⬤ SUN (Check One)

Scripture for Today: Read Mark 2:23–3:19

In today's reading Jesus got into trouble with the Pharisees because he _____
_____
_____
_____

I think the Pharisees made plans to kill Jesus *(v.3:6)* because _____
_____
_____
_____

Jesus' disciples chose to follow him. Some of the reasons I would be willing to be his disciple and follow him are _____

_____

_____

_____

_____

The Big Word: SOUL

Dictionary definition: _____

_____

_____

_____

If friends asked me to describe my "soul," I'd tell them that the soul is _____

_____

_____

_____

I believe that my soul will live forever with God!

◎ ● ● ● ● ● ● ● ● ● ● ◎
I agree 1 2 3 4 5 6 7 8 9 10 I disagree

(circle one)

Read 1 Thessalonians 5:23. I feel that my whole being, my spirit, soul, and body, can be free if _____

_____

_____

_____

My Prayer for Today

Dear God, thank you that you have created me with a soul that will live forever. Help me to be willing to _____

_____

_____

_____

Forgive me for the time that I _____
_____
_____
_____

I give you my soul, trusting that you will always _____
_____
_____
_____

Amen.

DAY 6: WEEK 1   ⬤ MON   ⬤ TUE   ⬤ WED   ⬤ THU   ⬤ FRI   ⬤ SAT   ⬤ SUN   (Check One)

Scripture for Today: Read Mark 3:20–35

In today's reading Jesus said, "Whoever does what God wants him to do is my brother, my sister, my mother." I think one thing that God wants me to do is _____
_____
_____
_____

The Big Word: PROMISE

Dictionary definition: _____
_____
_____

If someone breaks a promise he or she has made with me I feel _____
_____
_____

If I've made a promise to someone, it's important that I keep that promise because _____
_____
_____

Knowing that God has promised to love me always helps me to feel _____

_____

_____

_____

My Prayer for Today

Dear God, thank you that you have promised your love to us. I want to promise to you that I will _____

_____

_____

_____

As I continue this study, help me to _____

_____

_____

_____

Forgive me for the times when I _____

_____

_____

_____

_____

Amen.

DAY 7: WEEK 1   ● MON   ● TUE   ● WED   ● THU   ● FRI   ● SAT   ● SUN   (Check One)

Scripture for Today: Read Mark 4:1–20

Jesus used parables (stories) in order to _____

_____

_____

_____

_____

For me to "hear the message (of God)" and "accept it," like a seed in good soil, means that I am willing to _____

_____

_____

_____

The Big Word: GOD

Dictionary definition: _____

_____

_____

_____

Three words or phrases I would use to describe God are

1. _____

2. _____

3. _____

According to Genesis 1:1, God _____

_____

_____

_____

One question I have about God is _____

_____

_____

_____

My Prayer for Today

Dear God, thank you for creating the world and me in it! Six things in your creation I'm thankful for are

1. _____

2. _____

3. _____

4. _____

5. _____

6. _____

Three people in your creation I'm thankful for are
1. _____
2. _____
3. _____

As I continue to study more about Jesus, help me to _____
_____
_____
_____
_____

Amen.

CHAPTER 2

GOD HAS MADE PROMISES TO

_____

(Write your name here.)

DAY 1: WEEK 2 ● MON ● TUE ● WED ● THU ● FRI ● SAT ● SUN (Check One)

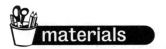 **materials**

Copies of _Bridges of Promise,_ Bibles, colored markers, and extra paper. Review Activity #3, "The Way I Picture God."

THE STORY: THE WAY I PICTURE GOD

The second class session took place in Pastor David's office at the church, a light and airy room with high ceilings and big windows. Pastor David's guitar leaned against one wall, and on another wall, a bulletin board displayed snapshots of friends, family, and mission trips he had participated in. Books crowded the shelves, papers cluttered the desk, and a pepperoni pizza jigsaw puzzle that Pastor David had glued to a board hung prominently near his desk. The office was like Pastor David himself, warm, friendly, and inviting.

This week's meeting started with ice cold milk and chocolate chip cookies, still warm from baking. Pastor Maria offered this prayer, "Dear God, thanks for simple gifts like these tasty cookies and refreshing milk. Thanks for the good feeling we have when we're together as friends here at this church. Teach us how to be your friends, dear God, and help us to know how much you love and care for us. In Jesus' name, Amen."

While the children ate their snacks, Pastor David asked them about their daily assignments to see how well they had done in completing all the reading and writing. They talked about some of the BIG WORDS and the questions the children had about the assignments.

discussion

Review the daily assignments and discuss each of the BIG WORDS. Talk about any questions that came up.

Pastor David was pleased that everyone had finished all of the assignments. "That's wonderful! We're off to a great start!" he exclaimed.

He removed a small box from one of his bookshelves, opened it, and said, "When I did my final paper, called a 'thesis,' in theological school, I went to the public schools to invite children from kindergarten through ninth grade to think about God and then draw their own pictures of God." He pulled some examples of the children's drawings from the cardboard box.

"I also asked them to write a description of God on the back of their drawings. Of course, the small children couldn't write, so I interviewed them with a tape recorder. Before I was done I had collected more than five hundred drawings of God. It was amazing how much I learned about how unique each child's drawing was."

Pastor David showed a few more examples to the class of some of the interesting drawings of God, and then he said, "That's what I'd like us to do today. Find Activity #3, entitled 'The Way I Picture God,' at the back of your book. Grab a pencil and some colored markers, take a moment to think about God, then start drawing. Remember that the idea isn't to show what great artists we are. Whatever you draw will be great, so have fun with the assignment."

activity

Parents/adult leaders, use a blank sheet of paper for your own drawing and description of God.

After a short while Pastor Maria said, "Some of you may be finishing before others, so when you're done with the drawing, turn the page over and write a description of God. When you're finished with that, wait until everyone else has finished."

When everyone had completed the project, Pastor David smiled and said to the group, "And now it's show-and-tell-time. I'll begin by showing you my drawing and telling you about it. Then you can each take a turn telling the rest of us about your picture."

 discussion

Show your drawings and read your descriptions to each other.

Pastor David had drawn a simple circle. He said, "To me, God is like a circle around everything and everyone. A circle is a line that has no beginning and no ending. That's the way I think about God. God always was, and God always will be. Amazing to think about, isn't it?"

Angela was next. She had drawn a stick person standing in the middle of big hands. "That's me,"she grinned, pointing to the stick figure. "I think of myself standing in the big, powerful, loving hands of God."

Daniel had drawn a picture of a man hanging on a cross. Bright red marks representing the blood of Jesus Christ ran down the cross. "I believe that when Jesus died on the cross, God showed us how much we are loved," Daniel said.

Esteban had drawn the lofty, snow-capped mountains in Guatemala. He explained, "I feel close to God when I'm in the mountains, because I realize how small I am and how huge and wonderful God is."

Tyrel had drawn dark clouds with lightning striking the ground, but he had added a colorful rainbow, too. "Whenever I hear thunder and watch the lightning, I think about how mysterious and powerful God is. I've always liked the story of Noah and how God promised never to destroy the earth with a flood again."

Joy had drawn a bearded man in a white robe helping children cross the street. "I believe God is like a very kind person who wants to help us."

And finally, Pastor Maria revealed her picture, a triangle with an eye in the middle. "I think of God as someone who knows all, sees all, and cares about all of creation. The triangle represents the three ways I like to think of God—God the Creator, God in Jesus Christ, and God the Holy Spirit."

Pastor David said, "What a wonderful gallery of religious art we've created here today! If you don't mind, I'd like to put your pictures on the bulletin board outside my office for a few weeks." The children were honored!

Pastor Maria introduced the next activity by saying, "The Bible has a lot to teach us about God. Let's take turns reading the following Scriptures, and then writing in our own words what the verses tell us about God."

Read Genesis 1:1, and then finish the sentence:
God is _____

_____

Read Genesis 2:7, and then finish the sentence:
God is _____

_____

Read Micah 6:8, and then finish the sentence:
God expects us to _____

_____

Read John 14:8–9, and then finish the sentence:
We know more about God because _____

_____

Read Ephesians 4:6, and then finish the sentence:
God is _____

_____

Read 1 John 4:8, and then finish the sentence:
God _____

_____

After the class had discussed each verse, the children took turns reading the story of Jesus in Mark 4:21–41, and then they wrote responses to the sentence completions.

Scripture for Today: Read Mark 4:21–41

Jesus said that the "Kingdom of God" is like _____

_____

_____

_____

_____

I believe Jesus had the power to calm the storm because _____
_____
_____
_____

As I get to know Jesus better, one thing I admire about him is that he _____
_____
_____
_____
_____

discussion

After the discussion of the story of Jesus, Pastor Maria announced the BIG WORD for the day. "Drum roll, please!" Everyone started clapping their legs. "And the BIG WORD for today is LOVE! Let's look up the definition of *love* in the dictionary." The children wrote the definition as their pastor read, and then they completed the sentences.

The Big Word: LOVE

Dictionary definition: _____
_____
_____
_____

I feel "loved" by people when they _____
_____
_____
_____

To say that I love someone means that I'm willing to _____
_____
_____
_____

To say that I love God means that I'm willing to _____
_____
_____
_____

Love may be the most important thing in the world because _____

_____

_____

_____

_____

discussion

As the group talked about the BIG WORD, Joy said, "I think of love as the good feeling I have when I go to my grandma's house. I've always felt love for my grandma, and I know she loves me, too."

Daniel added, "I'm not so sure love is always such a good feeling. I know my mom loves me, even when she tells me I have to go to my room for 'time out.' I guess she just wants to teach me what's best for me."

"I didn't even know how much I loved my Dad until he was gone. I think sometimes we take love for granted," Angela said.

And Tyrel said, "I know what you mean! When my parents got their divorce, it seemed so unfair to me. I couldn't understand how they could stop loving each other. Sometimes it felt like they stopped loving me, too. But I discovered after the divorce that they both loved me even more than ever."

Esteban had been quiet, thinking about what to say. "I believe that love is more than just a feeling. It's more like a promise to try to do my best to make life better for the people I love."

"Excellent, everyone!" Pastor Maria said. "We all need love in our lives. Let me tell you something personal. Life hasn't been easy for me, but I've believed all my life that the One who created me also loves me. And there is nothing I have ever done or ever can do that will keep God from loving me. I really believe in God's love."

"That's why Jesus came to earth," Pastor David continued. "People just didn't understand God's love, and they didn't know how to live God's way. They needed a teacher, someone to show them God's love. So God sent Jesus to be our teacher and leader, the one to help us discover more about God. A good friend of mine once told me that the difference between those who are Christian and those who aren't is not that God loves Christians any more than non-Christians. The difference is that Christians just know and believe God loves them."

Pastor David added, "If God loves us, even more than a grandma does, then we will never know how much we are loved, until we return our love to God. I think that's why Jesus taught us to love God with our whole hearts." Pastor David looked serious and joyful all at the same time. "If any of you are able to say, 'Yes, I know God loves me, and I love God with all my heart!' then you're ready to become a Christian—a disciple and follower of Jesus Christ."

Maria added, "David and I are hoping and praying that each of you will find the courage to make that choice and discover just how great it is to be a follower of Christ. We think it's the most important choice you'll ever make, because it will have a positive effect on all the other choices you make.

"We want you to think about all of this as you write your prayer for today. Let's take a few moments to write our prayers, and then I'll lead us in a closing prayer." The children were quiet and thoughtful as they began writing their prayers.

 activity

My Prayer for Today

Dear God, thank you that you have promised always to love me. And thank you that these are some of the people who love me: _____

_____
_____
_____
_____

Forgive me for the times when I fail to love (who?) _____

_____
_____
_____

And help me to love (who?) _____

_____
_____
_____
_____
_____

Amen.

When the children had finished writing, Pastor David invited everyone to join hands in a circle, and then he offered this closing prayer: "Dear God, help us to understand just how much you love us! Sometimes we don't honor you with our love. Forgive us. And help each of us to be willing to choose to follow Jesus Christ every day. Thank you that Jesus came to reveal your love to us and to teach us how to love one another. Thanks that we are growing in our love for each other in this group. In Jesus' name. Amen."

DAY 2: WEEK 2   ⬤ MON   ⬤ TUE   ⬤ WED   ⬤ THU   ⬤ FRI   ⬤ SAT   ⬤ SUN   (Check One)

Scripture for Today: Read Mark 5:1–20

If I had been the farmer who owned this herd of pigs, I would have _____
_____
_____
_____

I think it took a lot of courage for Jesus to _____
_____
_____
_____

The Big Word: HOLY SPIRIT

Dictionary definition of HOLY: _____
_____
_____
_____

Dictionary definition of SPIRIT: _____
_____
_____
_____

Jesus said the Spirit is like a wind blowing in the trees *(John 3:8)*. Some of the ways I think the Spirit of God is like the wind are _____
_____
_____
_____

Jesus also described the Spirit as a "helper" *(John 14:16)*. I have felt helped by the Spirit of God when _____
_____
_____
_____
_____

My Prayer for Today

*God, you have come to us in the form of the Holy Spirit to comfort and guide us.
Thank you for the way you have helped me to* _____

_____

_____

_____

Teach me how to _____

_____

_____

And please help me to be willing to _____

_____

_____

_____

Amen.

DAY 3: WEEK 2　● MON　● TUE　● WED　● THU　● FRI　● SAT　● SUN　(Check One)

Scripture for Today: Read Mark 5:21–43

If I had been twelve years old and Jesus had restored me to life, I think I would want to

_____

_____

_____

I'm amazed that Jesus _____

_____

_____

I wish I could ask Jesus why he _____

_____

_____

_____

The Big Word: JESUS

Dictionary definition: _____
_____
_____
_____

I believe Jesus is the Son of God

◎ • • • • • • • • • ◎
Not   1   2   3   4   5   6   7   8   9   10   No
sure   question
             (circle one)   about it

Explain: _____
_____
_____
_____
_____
_____
_____

Jesus showed his love for the world (and me) by _____
_____
_____
_____

I can show my love for Jesus by asking the question WWJWMTD? *(What would Jesus want me to do?)* One thing I'm not doing that I believe Jesus would want me to do is
_____
_____
_____

My Prayer for Today

Dear God, thank you that you gave yourself to the world when Jesus was born in Bethlehem. Help me to understand why _____
_____
_____
_____

And help me to believe that _____
_____
_____
_____

I want to be willing to _____
_____
_____
_____
_____

Amen.

DAY 4: WEEK 2 ● MON ● TUE ● WED ● THU ● FRI ● SAT ● SUN (Check One)

Scripture for Today: Read Mark 6:1–13

When Jesus sent out his twelve disciples, he told them to _____
_____
_____
_____

Why? _____
_____
_____
_____

One thing I like about Jesus is that he _____
_____
_____
_____

I wish I knew why Jesus _____
_____
_____
_____

The Big Word: SIN

Dictionary definition: _____
_____
_____
_____

If someone asked me, "What's sin?" I'd tell them that sin is _____
_____
_____
_____
_____

I'm not a "sinner" 1 2 3 4 5 6 7 8 9 10 I'm definitely a "sinner"

(circle one)

Explain: _____
_____
_____
_____
_____
_____

An example of something I have done that was a "sin" is _____
_____
_____
_____
_____
_____

This is what Romans 3:23 and Romans 6:23 teach me about "sin": _____
_____
_____
_____

According to 1 John 1:8–9, God expects us to _____
_____
_____
_____

My Prayer for Today

Dear God, I admit that I have sinned and fallen short of what you want me to be and do. For example, I know I have failed to _____
_____
_____
_____

And I've been unwilling to _____
_____
_____
_____

I know that one person I've hurt or done wrong to is _____
_____
_____
_____

Help me to make it right with that person by _____
_____
_____
_____

Thank you for your forgiveness. In Jesus' name, Amen.

DAY 5: WEEK 2   ● MON ● TUE ● WED ● THU ● FRI ● SAT ● SUN   (Check One)

Scripture for Today: Read Mark 6:14–44

John the Baptist was Jesus' cousin. If I had a relative or friend who was murdered by someone, I would feel _____
_____
_____

I think Jesus must have felt _____
_____
_____

If I had been in the hungry crowd and received food from Jesus, I would have thought that Jesus must be _____

_____

_____

_____

The Big Word: TEMPTATION

Dictionary definition: _____

_____

_____

_____

Sometimes I feel tempted to _____

_____

_____

_____

When we pray the Lord's prayer, we say, "Lead us not into temptation, but deliver us from evil." Some of the temptations that I know God would want me to avoid are _____

_____

_____

_____

I believe God will lead me away from these temptations, if I'm willing to _____

_____

_____

_____

My Prayer for Today

Dear God, when I am tempted to do what is wrong in your eyes, help me to _____

_____

_____

_____

And when I give in to temptation and go against you, forgive me for _____

_____

_____

Thank you for the many times you have _____
_____
_____
_____

In Jesus' name, Amen.

DAY 6: WEEK 2 ● MON ● TUE ● WED ● THU ● FRI ● SAT ● SUN (Check One)

Scripture for Today: Read Mark 6:45–56

If I had seen, with my own eyes, Jesus walking on the water, I would have thought ____
_____
_____
_____

Some of the things I admire about Jesus are _____
_____
_____
_____

The Big Word: DEATH

Dictionary definition: _____
_____
_____

If I knew that I would die one year from today, I think I'd want to be sure to _____
_____
_____
_____

Some people are afraid to die because they think _____
_____
_____

When it's time for me to die, I hope people will be able to say that I _____

_____

_____

_____

_____

My Prayer for Today

A child's bedtime prayer says, "Now I lay me down to sleep. I pray the Lord my soul to keep. If I should die before I wake, I pray the Lord my soul to take." Dear God, thank you that you love me enough so that when I do die, you will _____

_____

_____

_____

I want to be willing to love you enough to _____

_____

_____

_____

I promise that I will try to _____

_____

_____

_____

In Jesus' name, Amen.

DAY 7: WEEK 2 ● MON ● TUE ● WED ● THU ● FRI ● SAT ● SUN (Check One)

Scripture for Today: Read Mark 7:1–23

I'd like to ask Jesus why _____

_____

_____

_____

_____

Jesus teaches us that the things that make a person "unclean" are _____
_____
_____
_____

Something about Jesus I find hard to understand is _____
_____
_____
_____
_____
_____

The Big Word: SALVATION

Dictionary definition: _____
_____
_____
_____

If I couldn't swim and fell into a river, I would need to have someone "save me" from drowning. In that case "salvation" means that _____
_____
_____
_____

If someone did rescue me from death, I would feel _____
_____
_____

To say that "Jesus saves me from eternal death," means that he _____
_____
_____
_____

Ephesians 2:8–9 tells me that I'm saved not because of what I do, but because God has
_____
_____

My Prayer for Today

Thank you, dear God, for offering salvation to me if I'm willing to believe in your Son, Jesus Christ.

I believe that I have sinned and need your forgiveness. (check one)

⚪ *yes* ⚪ *no* ⚪ *not yet*

I believe Jesus is the one who has rescued and saved me from sin and death.

⚪ *yes* ⚪ *no* ⚪ *not yet*

Jesus, I am willing to receive the gift of your love, grace, and salvation.

⚪ *yes* ⚪ *no* ⚪ *not yet*

Thank you for the gift of your salvation. In Jesus' name, Amen.

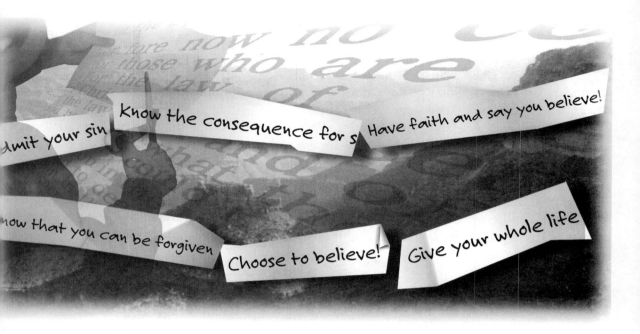

Admit your sin

Know the consequence for s

Have faith and say you believe!

now that you can be forgiven

Choose to believe!

Give your whole life

CHAPTER 3

JESUS IS THE BRIDGE FROM

_____

(Write your name here.)

TO GOD

DAY 1: WEEK 3   ⬤ MON ⬤ TUE ⬤ WED ⬤ THU ⬤ FRI ⬤ SAT ⬤ SUN   (Check One)

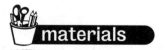 **materials**

Copies of *Bridges of Promise,* Bibles, pencils, scissors, and tape. Before the class begins, label two chairs, one "God" and the other "People." Review Activity #4, "Steps on the Bridge to God."

THE STORY: THE BRIDGE FROM PEOPLE TO GOD

Pastors Maria and David decided to hold the third class session in a room at the church where one of the walls has a huge picture showing Jesus as he hangs on the cross. The popcorn and cans of soda pop were waiting for the children as they entered the room. It was like a party to see everyone again!

"Let's begin our session with prayer," Pastor David said as the children bowed their heads. "Dear God, thanks for our refreshment today, and thanks for the progress we are making toward knowing one another a lot better. Most of all today we want to thank you for Jesus Christ and his willingness to die for us on the cross. We welcome you to our meeting and are glad that your Spirit is with us here. Amen."

As the children continued to munch their popcorn, Pastor Maria asked how they had done with their daily assignments, and if anyone had questions about the work.

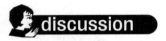

Take time to review the daily work now.

Then, Pastor Maria said, "David and I decided to have the class in this room because of that large painting. Have you ever noticed it?"

Esteban said, "I noticed it the first time I visited this church. A lot of churches in Guatemala have paintings like that. I like it, because it helps me remember why the church is here."

"Esteban's right!" Pastor David said, "The church wouldn't exist and none of us would even be sitting here today learning about Jesus if he had not been willing to die on the cross. Take a minute to study the painting, and then tell me how it makes you feel."

The class was silent as they stared at the painting. Then Angela said, "A picture like that makes me feel sad. It seems like such a cruel way to die."

Tyrel added, "It makes me feel sad, too, but it also makes me feel thankful."

"Thankful?"

"Yes, thankful that God loved us so much."

Daniel said, "I can't imagine how painful it must have been for Jesus. It seems like an awful way to die."

"And what's even more amazing," Pastor Maria added, "is that Jesus was no ordinary person. He was the Son of God—a perfect human being. He didn't deserve to die like that. But Jesus loved God with all of his heart, mind, soul, and body and was willing to do whatever was necessary to show God's love for the world. It's an amazing story!"

Pastor David invited the children to find chapter 3 and said, "Now look at the session title: 'Jesus is the Bridge from _____ to God.' Write your name on the line."

"Today we want to talk about why Jesus died for each one of us, and what a difference he can make in our lives. Did you notice the two chairs when you came in the room? We're going to build a bridge from the back of one chair to the back of the other. Did you notice the labels? One chair represents 'People' and the other, 'God.' The bridge we're going to build shows some of the steps we need to take in understanding how Jesus helps us to come to God.

"So turn to Activity #4 at the back of your book, and use your scissors to start cutting the planks we'll be using to build our bridge." Pastor David assigned each child one or two sections to cut out and asked them to be ready to read the Scripture on their section(s) when it was time.

 activity   discussion

Tyrel was first and read Romans 3:22–23. After the group discussed the idea that we have to "admit our sin," Tyrel taped the first plank to the section of the bridge nearest to the chair labeled "People." Daniel took the next plank, Angela the third, and so on until all bridge planks were attached and hanging between the two chairs, and all the Scriptures had been discussed.

Pastor Maria said, "Excellent job! You're good bridge builders. These are all good Bible verses to help us understand the steps in becoming followers of Jesus Christ. Now let me ask you a question. Do you remember the story of Adam and Eve in the garden?"

Joy had heard the story many times and raised her hand. "God created Adam and Eve and gave them this beautiful place to live, the Garden of Eden. Then, God said they could eat whatever they were hungry for in the garden, but not the fruit of the tree in the center of the garden."

Pastor Maria interrupted, "Thanks, Joy. Someone else can continue the story."

Tyrel raised his hand and said, "Satan, in the form of a snake, tempted Eve to eat the fruit, and then Adam ate it, too."

"What happened next?"

"They hid in the bushes," Daniel said. "I think it was because they knew that they had broken God's rule and were afraid God would punish them."

"And so their disobedience and sin hurt their relationship with God, didn't it?" Pastor Maria continued. "That's what happens, isn't it? Sin destroys life and relationships. In fact, sin tends to hurt every part of life—mind, body, soul, and heart. But the really neat thing about God's promise to us is that if we admit we are sinners and ask to be forgiven, God will always forgive us and renew our relationship."

Pastor David pointed to the "People" chair and said, "We find ourselves on one side of a deep canyon. It's the canyon of broken rules and promises that haven't been kept. We tend to do our own thing rather than what God wants. And on the other side of the 'canyon of sin,' God waits for us and invites us to cross over to life and right relationship. With God, all that's necessary is that we admit our sin, say we're sorry, then live our lives for Jesus."

Pastor Maria pointed to the picture of Jesus on the wall and said, "It's hard for all of us to understand why Jesus had to die on the cross, but I think our relationship with God was so important that Jesus, God's only Son, needed to die on the cross to become a way for us to be forgiven. It's an incredible gift!"

"I think I'm beginning to get it!" Daniel said. "It's through Jesus that people come to God, but I've got to decide that I will believe in Jesus and live my life for him, don't I?"

"That's exactly it, Daniel!" Pastor Maria was excited. "And that's the invitation I want you all to think about. Consider giving your life—all of your heart, mind, soul, and body—to God. Believe in Jesus, confess your sin, and promise to live your life for Jesus. I made that promise years ago, and it's changed how I live my life in a very positive way."

Angela looked confused, "But how do we do it? If you want to cross the bridge to God but don't know how to do it, how do you get started across the bridge?"

"It's not all that complicated," Pastor Maria said. "In fact, a lot of people miss it because they think it's harder than it really is. Angela, when you're ready to commit your life to Jesus Christ and make that promise, all you need to do is tell God. Speak your mind and heart to God in a prayer."

"I wouldn't know what to say," Angela said. "I'm not very good at praying out loud."

"You don't need to pray out loud," Pastor David said. "In fact, we can pray right now, and for any of you who think you're ready to make that promise, just pray along in your heart and soul. If you're not ready yet, that's okay. Just think about the prayer as I lead. Let's all close our eyes and concentrate on God who, I believe, is listening to us right now, and hears what we're saying and thinking."

activity

Invite any in the group who are willing to promise to live their life for Jesus Christ—heart, mind, soul, and body—to pray with Pastor David and the other children.

The children were very quiet and reverent as they closed their eyes tight, and Pastor David guided them in prayer: "First, admit that you have sinned and not always lived up to what God wants you to be and do. Think about specific times when you know you fell short of what God wanted you to be or do, and tell God that you're sorry." Pastor David waited while the children prayed silently.

"Next, accept God's forgiveness. Picture Jesus Christ on the cross and believe that he died for you so that you would not have to pay the penalty for sin, eternal death." Pastor David waited.

"Now, promise that you will give your whole self—your heart (emotions and desires), your mind (thoughts and attitudes and choices), your soul (and personality), your body—your whole being and life to God. Promise that you will try to do your best to love and obey God and follow the teachings of Jesus." Pastor David paused.

And so, in front of the picture of the one who died on the cross, the children, each in their own way, offered their lives to Jesus. They received forgiveness and believed in the miracle of God's love. They made their own promises to God.

After a long pause, Pastor David said "Amen" and the children opened their eyes, half expecting the world to look different, but the room and every person in it looked just as it had before the prayer. Just then, the afternoon sun poured through the window into the room, and a beam of light illuminated the dark picture of the Christ hanging on the cross. The sun's brilliance and warmth was like the promise of God to be present at all times, and everyone felt a warmth inside, the good feeling that comes when you know you've made the right choice.

Pastor David said, "That was spectacular!" and reached for his Bible. "It's time now to read the continuing story of Jesus from Mark 7:24–37, so let's look in our Bibles and take turns reading the verses." After reading, the children wrote their response to the sentence completion that followed.

Scripture for Today: Read Mark 7:24–37

The more I read about the things that Jesus did, the more I believe that Jesus _____
_____
_____
_____

The woman had faith to believe that Jesus could _____
_____
_____
_____
_____

I have faith to believe that Jesus can help me to _____
_____
_____
_____

After their discussion of the story, Pastor Maria announced that it was time for the BIG WORD! "Drum roll, please! And the BIG WORD is FAITH! David's going to demonstrate faith to all of us."

"But I need a volunteer." Pastor David said, and Daniel raised his hand. "Okay, Daniel, stand in front of me with your back to me. Close your eyes tight. Now I promise to catch you when you fall backward into my arms."

 activity

Try this activity yourself.

Daniel fell backward, and sure enough, Pastor David caught him. "That's what faith is. It's trusting in God's promise to catch us and keep us from falling. God wants to save us from being hurt, if we will only trust in the promises of God."

Pastor David added, "There was no way Daniel could know for sure that I would catch him. I could have let him fall to the floor, but I didn't, because I had promised. Daniel believed my promise. He gave himself—heart, mind, soul, and body—to believe that I wouldn't let him down."

Pastor Maria invited the children to write the definition to the BIG WORD as she read from Webster. Then the children completed the section on faith and discussed their answers.

 activity

The Big Word: FAITH

Dictionary definition: _____

_____

_____

_____

If I sit on a chair, I have faith (trust) that the chair will hold me up. If that's true, then "to have faith in God" means that I trust and believe that God will _____

_____

_____

_____

According to Hebrews 11:1–3, faith is _____

_____

_____

_____

Some things I know are "real," even if I can't see them with my eyes, are _____

_____

_____

_____

_____

As the discussion drew to a close, Pastor David said, "Let's bring our class to a conclusion today by writing our own prayers."

My Prayer for Today

Dear God, I have faith and believe that you are _____
_____
_____
_____
_____

Thank you that I am learning to trust in your ability to _____
_____
_____
_____
_____

Thank you that you have helped me to _____
_____
_____
_____
_____
_____

Amen.

When all had finished writing, Pastor Maria invited the children to stand in a circle. "If any of you would like to read your prayer to the rest of us, you're welcome to do so now." After each child had taken a turn praying, Pastor Maria said this closing prayer: "What a wonderful time we've had, dear God, thinking about Jesus Christ as our bridge to you. Thank you that I made a promise to you a long time ago to believe in Jesus. And thanks for the many ways you have helped me grow in my faith through the years. I especially thank you for each of my friends and the promises they have made to you today. Help us all to have the courage to keep our faith promises to you and trust that you will love us forever! Amen."

DAY 2: WEEK 3 ⬤ MON ⬤ TUE ⬤ WED ⬤ THU ⬤ FRI ⬤ SAT ⬤ SUN (Check One)

Scripture for Today: Read Mark 8:1–21

If I had been in the crowd that Jesus fed, I would have thought that Jesus _____

_____

_____

_____

Jesus was a person who _____

_____

_____

_____

_____

I'm amazed that Jesus _____

_____

_____

_____

_____

The Big Word: LORD

Dictionary definition: _____

_____

_____

_____

To accept that Jesus is the "Lord of my life" means that I am willing to let him _____

_____

_____

_____

Read John 20:26–29. When Thomas said "My Lord and my God" to Jesus after the resurrection, I think Thomas really believed that Jesus was _____

_____

_____

_____

Even though I've never seen Jesus with my eyes, I'm coming to believe that Jesus is ____

_____

_____

_____

My Prayer for Today

Dear Lord, thank you for helping me to understand that Jesus is _____

_____

_____

_____

I'm willing to let you be the Lord, master and leader of my life and future.

    ○ *yes* ○ *no* ○ *not yet*

Help me to _____

_____

_____

_____

In Jesus' name, Amen.

DAY 3: WEEK 3   ● MON ● TUE ● WED ● THU ● FRI ● SAT ● SUN   (Check One)

Scripture for Today: Read Mark 8:22–38

If I could, I'd like to ask the blind man _____

_____

_____

_____

If Jesus asked me, "Who do you say that I am?" I'd say, "You are _____

_____

_____

_____

Reread verse 35. This is what the verse means to me _____
_____
_____
_____

The Big Word: SAVIOR

Dictionary definition: _____
_____
_____
_____

I believe Jesus is called our "savior" because he _____
_____
_____
_____

Refer to Romans 3:23 again. The Bible teaches us Jesus died on the cross in order to save us. When I believe in Jesus as my Lord and Savior, I am saved from what? _____
_____
_____
_____

Read Ephesians 2:10. If we are saved from the result of sin (eternal death), then why are we given eternal life in Christ? _____
_____
_____
_____

My Prayer for Today

Dear God, today I'm especially thankful for Jesus and his willingness to be my savior. Help me to understand why _____
_____
_____
_____

Thank you for _____
_____
_____

Forgive me today for _____

_____

_____

Thank you for being my Lord and Savior! Amen.

DAY 4: WEEK 3   ● MON   ● TUE   ● WED   ● THU   ● FRI   ● SAT   ● SUN   (Check One)

Scripture for Today: Read Mark 9:1–29

If I had heard the voice in the cloud *(v. 7)*, I would have believed more than ever that Jesus

_____

_____

_____

If I had been the boy's father, I would have _____

_____

_____

The Big Word: DISCIPLE

Dictionary definition: _____

_____

_____

_____

If a disciple is a student who is loyal to his or her teacher, then for me to be a disciple of Jesus Christ means that I _____

_____

_____

_____

Some of the things Jesus wants me to learn about living life are _____

_____

_____

_____

Some of the ways I can learn more about the teachings of Jesus are _____
_____
_____
_____

According to Matthew 28:19–20, Jesus wants his followers to _____
_____
_____
_____

My Prayer for Today

Dear God, I want to be a good student and disciple of Jesus, so help me to _____
_____
_____
_____

Thank you for some of the people in my life who have taught me, including _____
_____
_____
_____

Today I'm thankful to you for many things, including _____
_____
_____
_____

Help me to make Jesus the most important teacher in my life. Amen.

DAY 5: WEEK 3　● MON　● TUE　● WED　● THU　● FRI　● SAT　● SUN　(Check One)

Scripture for Today: Read Mark 9:30–50

Jesus said we are "great" when we serve others. Some of the people who "serve" me are
_____
_____
_____

Some of the people I serve are _____
_____
_____

I could do more to serve others by _____
_____
_____
_____

One verse in today's reading that is hard for me to understand is verse _____
because _____
_____
_____

The Big Word: GRACE

Dictionary definition: _____
_____
_____
_____

When I hear the song "Amazing Grace," I think "grace" is _____
_____
_____
_____

When the Bible talks about "grace," it suggests that even though we don't earn it by doing good things, God loves us and forgives us anyway. Ephesians 2:8–10 tells me that grace is amazing because _____
_____
_____
_____

My Prayer for Today

Dear God, thank you for the amazing way you have accepted and loved me even when I didn't deserve it. Forgive me for these sins _____
_____
_____

Help me to understand why _____

_____

_____

_____

In Jesus' name, Amen.

DAY 6: WEEK 3 ● MON ● TUE ● WED ● THU ● FRI ● SAT ● SUN (Check One)

Scripture for Today: Read Mark 10:1–31

Jesus loved little children and blessed them. A person I know who loves and blesses me is

_____

_____

_____

And I know this because he or she _____

_____

_____

_____

I think the rich man responded to Jesus the way he did because _____

_____

_____

_____

It might be hard for rich people to be disciples of Jesus because _____

_____

_____

_____

The Big Word: BELIEVE

Dictionary definition: _____

_____

_____

I strongly believe that _____

_____

_____

_____

_____

To say I believe in something or someone means that I _____

_____

_____

_____

_____

To say that "I believe in Jesus Christ" means that I _____

_____

_____

_____

_____

Read John 3:16 again. The way to find eternal life is to believe in _____

_____

_____

_____

_____

My Prayer for Today

Dear God, I believe you are _____

_____

_____

_____

And I believe that you want me to _____

_____

_____

_____

Therefore, I'm willing to _____

_____

_____

_____

Please, help me to _____

_____

_____

_____

_____

And thank you for _____

_____

_____

_____

_____

In Jesus' name, Amen.

DAY 7: WEEK 3 ● MON ● TUE ● WED ● THU ● FRI ● SAT ● SUN   (Check One)

Scripture for Today: Read Mark 10:32–52

Jesus would say that if you want to be a great person, you need to be willing to *(v. 43)*

_____

_____

_____

_____

_____

When Jesus said that the blind man's faith made him well, I think he meant _____

_____

_____

_____

_____

After the blind man could see, he _____

_____

_____

_____

_____

The Big Word: ETERNITY

Dictionary definition: _____
_____
_____
_____

Human life has its beginning (birth) and its ending (death). To say that God is "eternal" means that God _____
_____
_____
_____

When John 3:16 says that if we believe in Jesus Christ we'll have everlasting or eternal life, I think it means that if I believe in Jesus Christ, when I die I will _____
_____
_____
_____

One question I have about eternity is _____
_____
_____
_____
_____
_____

My Prayer for Today

Thank you, dear God, for offering to me the gift of spending life and eternity with you. Help me to understand why _____
_____
_____
_____
_____

I promise that I will try to _____
_____
_____
_____
_____

Thank you, also, for helping me to understand that Jesus _____
_____
_____
_____
_____

In Jesus' name, Amen.

JESUS CHRIST INVITES

(Write your name here.)

TO BE A MEMBER OF HIS CHURCH

DAY 1: WEEK 4   ⬤ MON ⬤ TUE ⬤ WED ⬤ THU ⬤ FRI ⬤ SAT ⬤ SUN   (Check One)

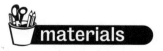 **materials**

Copies of *Bridges of Promise*, Bibles, pencils, and paint materials (yellow and blue paints, brushes and paper for painting). Review Activity #5, "What Makes a Church Baptist?"

THE STORY: WHEN GOD MIXES WITH US

For the fourth session, the children met in their own Sunday school classroom. When they arrived, they noticed that their pastors had set up a painting easel in the room.

As the children enjoyed the snack for the day, sliced apples with caramel topping,

Pastor Maria wrote the word *church* at the top of a sheet of newsprint and announced the chapter title for the day: "'Jesus Christ Invites _____ to Be a Member of His Church.' Find chapter 4 in your book and write your name in the title, because today we'll be talking about what it means for us to be members of Christ's church. To start, I need a volunteer." She handed a paintbrush and a bottle of yellow paint to Joy.

"What do you want me to do with this?" she asked.

"I'd like you to help us paint the church, but first I need a second painter." Pastor Maria handed another paintbrush and bottle of blue paint to Daniel. "Now Joy and Daniel, what will happen when you mix the blue and yellow together?"

"We'll get green," Daniel said.

"Okay, let's watch," Pastor Maria said as the two took their brushes and smeared the two colors on the paper, mixing them together. Green miraculously appeared on the page.

"Green is the color of life, isn't it?" Pastor David continued the lesson. "Think about it. If the yellow represents the presence of God and blue represents us, what happens when God mixes with us?"

Tyrel was catching on. "You get life!" he said.

"Absolutely!" Pastor David said. "The church is a group of people who believe that they get their life from God. And great things happen when God's Spirit mixes with us. When we decide to believe in Jesus Christ and accept him as our bridge to God, God's spirit mixes with ours. We become like new people. We're given new life. The Bible calls this eternal life with God. It's an amazing miracle!"

Pastor Maria carefully placed the brushes in a cup of water, twisted the paint jar lids back on, and said, "Now let me ask all of you a question that may take a lot of thought. How is that green splotch of paint a picture of First Baptist Church?" Joy raised her hand and said, "Our church is a group of people who have new life in Christ!"

"Exactly!" Pastor Maria said. "We all know that the church is more than a building, although we often talk about 'going to the church.' The church is a group of people who have chosen to give their lives to God and let the life, spirit, and love of Jesus Christ mix with their lives."

"See this?" Pastor David formed a tight fist with his hand and said, "When we are closed to God, our body, mind, spirit, and relationships are closed, too. But as we begin to open up to the promises of God,"—he slowly opened his fist—"we begin to open up our heart and lives to other people. It's a beautiful thing, like a flower opening to the sunshine."

"I think David would agree with me that it was our faith in Jesus Christ that helped the two of us to be more open to the love we discovered in each other," Pastor Maria said. "We wouldn't be married today, if we didn't both have faith in Jesus. We need to find people of faith who can help us become more of what God wants us to be."

Angela asked, "I have a question about church membership. If I want to join First Baptist, how do I do it?"

Pastor David said, "First, promise to be a lifetime follower of Jesus Christ."

Angela continued, "I've made that promise, but that doesn't mean I'm a member of First Baptist, does it?" For the first time in her life, Angela and the others in the room really wanted to know more about being members of their church.

"You're right, Angela," Pastor Maria said. "You're not officially a member of our church, not yet, but you're not far from it. The first step is promising to follow Jesus, and the next step is coming forward at the end of a worship service to let everyone know you have made that promise and want to be baptized. After you are baptized, the church welcomes you into membership. It's a simple process, but it's very important that you're sure you want to become a member."

Pastor David said, "Before any of you decide to become members of a Baptist church, it's important that we talk about some of the beliefs of Baptists. So right now, I'd like to give you a little quiz. Take out Activity #5, 'What Makes a Church Baptist?' and mark whether you think each statement is true or false. When you're finished, we'll discuss the statements together."

activity

The class went to work on the quiz. They were interested in knowing more about what made their church a Baptist church.

After everyone had completed the quiz, Pastors Maria and David started the discussion by announcing that all of the statements were true about Baptists. They talked about each statement and why it was so important.

discussion

Then Pastor Maria said, "These are some of the most important principles of our faith. For centuries now, Baptists have cherished these beliefs and made them the standard by which we call ourselves 'Baptist.'"

"There's a second part to the quiz," Pastor David announced, "only this time it's a fill-in-the-blanks that we'll do together. Turn your activity sheets over and let's talk about our church for a little while."

activity   **discussion**

If you're doing this activity at home and have questions that remain unanswered, plan to call the pastor or another church leader to get more information.

After their discussion about First Baptist, Pastor David invited the children to turn to the daily activity. The children took turns reading the story of Jesus in the Gospel of Mark (Mark 11:1–19) and responding to the questions that followed.

Scripture for Today: Read Mark 11:1–19

If I had been in the crowd when Jesus rode the donkey into Jerusalem, I would have thought he was _____

_____

_____

_____

Jesus turned over the tables of the moneychangers in the temple because _____

_____

_____

_____

Read verse 18 again. I think they wanted to kill Jesus because _____

_____

_____

_____

When they had completed their discussion, Pastor Maria announced, "And now the BIG WORD for today! Drum roll, everyone!" The class followed the tradition of beating out a loud drum roll on the classroom table. "Today's BIG WORD is, CHURCH! Let me ask you one more time, what is the church?"

Esteban smiled and pointed to their newsprint painting. "A green splotch of paint?"

"Yes, wise guy. But what does that green splotch of paint represent?" Pastor Maria persisted with a smile.

"Life!" the class chimed in, and Tyrel added, "Life in Christ!"

"Great!" Pastor Maria said. "So we are the church, if we believe in Jesus Christ and live as his followers. Don't ever forget it! The church is not the building. It's the people who believe in Jesus!"

Pastor David opened the dictionary and read the definition as the children wrote under the BIG WORD. Then they continued to complete the sentences under the word CHURCH.

activity

The Big Word: CHURCH

Dictionary definition: _____

_____

_____

_____

The church is more than a building. The church is _____
_____
_____
_____

Some of the things I like about the church I attend are _____
_____
_____
_____

If a church is to be healthy and strong, the members of the church need to be willing to
_____
_____
_____

discussion

After their discussion about the church, Pastor David invited the children to write their prayers for the day.

activity

My Prayer for Today

Thank you, God, for the church. I'm especially thankful for some of these people who are a part of the church where I attend: _____
_____
_____
_____

Help me to be willing to make my church stronger and healthier by _____
_____
_____
_____
_____

Thank you that you have invited me to be one of the disciples of Jesus and one of the members of his church.
Amen.

As another class time came to an end, Pastor Maria closed the class session with this prayer: "Dear God, once again we've had a wonderful time being the church together today. Your Spirit has mixed with ours. We are growing in our love for each other and our love for Jesus. Help each of us to understand the importance of your church in this world. Help us all to be faithful members of your church. In the precious name of our friend Jesus, our bridge to you. Amen."

DAY 2: WEEK 4 ⬤ MON ⬤ TUE ⬤ WED ⬤ THU ⬤ FRI ⬤ SAT ⬤ SUN (Check One)

Scripture for Today: Read Mark 11:20–33

I believe Jesus had so much authority and power because _____

_____

_____

_____

Something I learned about Jesus in today's reading is _____

_____

_____

_____

I wish I knew why Jesus _____

_____

_____

_____

_____

The Big Word: WORSHIP

Dictionary definition: _____

_____

_____

_____

If someone asked me, "Why is it important to worship God?" I'd tell that person _____

_____

_____

_____

The parts of our worship service that help me to feel close to God are _____

_____

_____

_____

We talk about the "worship service." Who are we serving when we come to worship?

_____

_____

_____

How are we serving? _____

_____

_____

_____

My Prayer for Today

Dear Lord, thank you that I can worship you.
You are wonderful and precious, so I praise you for _____

_____

_____

_____

And I thank you for _____

_____

_____

_____

I want to worship you with my heart, mind, soul, and body. Help me when I get together with others to worship you to be able to _____

_____

_____

_____

In Jesus' name, Amen.

DAY 3: WEEK 4 [● MON ● TUE ● WED ● THU ● FRI ● SAT ● SUN] (Check One)

Scripture for Today: Read Mark 12:1–17

People were often "amazed" at Jesus and at the things he said, such as *(v. 17)* _____
_____
_____
_____

What do I owe God? *(v. 17)* _____
_____
_____
_____

Reading Mark and the story of Jesus has helped me to _____
_____
_____
_____

The Big Word: FELLOWSHIP

Dictionary definition: _____
_____
_____
_____

Fellowship is another word for the friendship we have with other Christians because we all believe in Jesus Christ. A Christian friend I have fellowship with is _____
_____
_____

Some of the things that help the different age groups in our church know each other and experience fellowship and friendship are _____
_____
_____
_____

In the church I can still love a person I may not even like because _____
_____
_____
_____

My Prayer for Today

Dear God, thank you for others in my church who love me, including _____
_____
_____
_____

Help me to show friendship to others in my church by reaching out to _____
_____
_____
_____

Help everyone in our church to be willing to _____
_____
_____
_____

Thank you for my church. In Jesus' name, Amen.

DAY 4: WEEK 4   ● MON   ● TUE   ● WED   ● THU   ● FRI   ● SAT   ● SUN   (Check One)

Scripture for Today: Read Mark 12:18–44

According to Jesus the two most important rules for living are

1. _____
_____

2. _____
_____
_____

One of the things I love about Jesus is that he _____

_____

_____

_____

_____

The Big Word: SERVANT

Dictionary definition: _____

_____

_____

_____

Read Mark 10:43–45. Jesus asked his followers to serve others. A person who comes to my mind when I think about someone who serves others is _____

_____

_____

_____

and that's because he or she _____

_____

_____

_____

To be a "servant" means that I'm willing to _____

_____

_____

_____

Ways that I can serve my family include _____

_____

_____

_____

Some ways that I can serve God are _____

_____

_____

_____

My Prayer for Today

Dear God, I want to love others by serving them. Thank you that Jesus served and helped others by _____

_____

_____

_____

Forgive me for the times I'm unwilling to serve and help, for example: _____

_____

_____

_____

Thank you for the many people who serve God in my church, including _____

_____

_____

_____

_____

In Jesus' name, Amen.

DAY 5: WEEK 4   ⬤ MON ⬤ TUE ⬤ WED ⬤ THU ⬤ FRI ⬤ SAT ⬤ SUN   (Check One)

Scripture for Today: Read Mark 13:1–23

When I think about the "end of the world" and the "last days" it makes me feel _____

_____

_____

_____

_____

and I sometimes wonder if _____

_____

_____

_____

One thing I learned about Jesus from today's reading is that he _____
_____
_____
_____

If I could tell my friends what I think of Jesus, I'd tell them that Jesus _____
_____
_____
_____

The Big Word: WITNESS

Dictionary definition: _____
_____
_____
_____

To be a "witness" in a court of law means that I _____
_____
_____
_____

To be a "witness" for Jesus Christ means that I'm willing to tell others _____
_____
_____
_____

The name "Christian" means "little Christ." I am a "little Christ" to others whenever I
_____
_____
_____

My Prayer for Today

Dear God, thank you for the people in my life who have told me about Jesus, for example: _____
_____
_____
_____

Help me to be willing to be a witness and to tell others that Jesus _____

_____

_____

_____

A person I know who does not go to church anywhere is _____

_____

_____

_____

Please give me the courage to invite this person and to tell him or her about my faith in Jesus Christ. In Jesus' name, Amen.

DAY 6: WEEK 4   ● MON ● TUE ● WED ● THU ● FRI ● SAT ● SUN   (Check One)

Scripture for Today: Read Mark 13:24–37

If someone asked me, "When do you think the world will end?" I'd tell him or her that according to the Bible _____

_____

_____

_____

One question I have about the future is _____

_____

_____

_____

_____

The Big Word: MEMBER

Dictionary definition: _____

_____

_____

_____

I feel I'm a member and belong to a group if _____

_____

_____

A person who helps me to feel that I belong in my church is _____

_____

_____

because he or she _____

_____

_____

_____

Some of the reasons it is a good idea to become an official member of my church are

_____

_____

_____

Before I become a member of my church, I'll need to _____

_____

_____

_____

My Prayer for Today

Dear God, thank you for the members of my church. As I think about becoming a member of my church, help me to _____

_____

_____

_____

Thank you that you love me. Help me to show my love for you by _____

_____

_____

_____

Forgive me for the times that I'm not willing to _____

_____

_____

_____

Thank you for _____

_____

_____

_____

In Jesus' name, Amen.

DAY 7: WEEK 4 ● MON ● TUE ● WED ● THU ● FRI ● SAT ● SUN (Check One)

Scripture for Today: Read Mark 14:1–21

The woman who poured perfume on Jesus' head must have wanted to show Jesus ____

_____

_____

_____

Some people criticized her because _____

_____

_____

_____

But Jesus received her gift by saying _____

_____

_____

One way I'd like to be more like Jesus is in the way I _____

_____

_____

_____

The Big Word: PRAYER

Dictionary definition: _____

_____

_____

_____

If someone asked me, "What is prayer?" I'd say that prayer is _____
_____
_____
_____

Taking time to pray is a valuable thing to do because _____
_____
_____
_____

Lately, I've been praying that _____
_____
_____
_____

One question I have about prayer is _____
_____
_____

My Prayer for Today

Dear God, I want to thank you for many things, including _____
_____
_____
_____

As I think about a challenge I'm facing, please God, help me to _____
_____
_____

As I think about others I know who need your help right now, please help _____
_____
_____
_____

In Jesus' name, Amen.

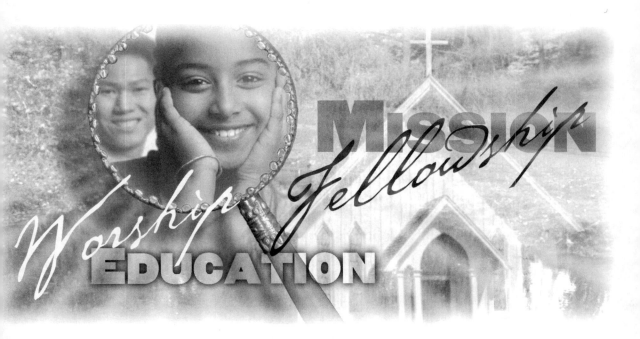

CHAPTER 5

_____'s
(Write your name here.)

PROMISE TO THE CHURCH

DAY 1: WEEK 5   ● MON ● TUE ● WED ● THU ● FRI ● SAT ● SUN   (Check One)

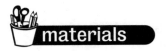

Copies of *Bridges of Promise*, Bibles, pencils, scissors, colored markers, and tape. Review Activity #6, "The Church."

THE STORY: THE CHURCH IS A MOUNTAIN OF PROMISE

When the children arrived, they followed the arrows to Pastor Maria's office, the office right next to Pastor David's office. The children wondered what the snack would be, but there was no food in sight when they arrived.

Daniel was curious. "What's to eat? I'm kind of hungry!"

"It's a surprise," Pastor David said as he motioned for everyone to follow. "Come on! Let's go into the kitchen to see what treasures we can find!"

They walked the long hallway to the kitchen, flicked on the lights, and when Pastor David opened the door to the freezer, they discovered the treasure—ice cream bars! What a great feeling to stand in the kitchen talking and laughing as they ate and talked. Everyone could see now why being a part of the fellowship of a church youth group can be one of the best things life has to offer.

Back in Pastor Maria's office, the children noticed a beautifully wrapped package that she had placed on the floor. She said, "The title for today is '_____'s Promise to the Church,' so write your name in the title for chapter 5."

activity

As they wrote, Pastor Maria said, "We've talked a lot about the promise to give our hearts, minds, souls, and bodies to God. It's our way of showing love for God. But aren't there also some promises we need to make to the church?"

Tyrel raised his hand. "We need to be here, otherwise we'd miss out on all the good stuff that goes on—like ice cream bars! Attendance is important!"

"And giving money is important, too," Joy added.

Esteban said, "And helping whenever we can! Like cleaning up the kitchen after we finish eating the snack."

And Daniel said, "Being friendly to new people who come."

Angela added, "Being friendly to everyone—even people we may not even like."

Pastor Maria said, "Thanks for saying that, Angela, because it leads right into the poem that I want to read today. But before I read, would someone like to open the present that's on the floor. How about you, Esteban?"

Esteban read the tag to the group, "My gift to the church," and started to remove the paper and bow. He opened the lid to a shoe box, and when he looked inside, he smiled. Inside the box he saw himself smiling back. Pastor Maria had taped a mirror in the bottom of the box!

"Esteban, show the gift to the rest of the group," Pastor Maria said. Esteban carried the shoe box around the circle, giving everyone a chance to look inside.

Pastor Maria said, "That's our most important gift to the church, isn't it? We give ourselves, don't we? We give our hearts, minds, souls, and bodies, not only to God, but also to one another. Now I'd like to read a poem I wrote when I was in seminary studying to be a pastor. It's about how we're each a gift to God and to one another."

> We are gifts of God.
> Other persons are gifts that God sends to us.
> Some are beautifully wrapped inside attractive paper,

Others come wrapped in very ordinary paper.
But all are attractive to God.

The wrapping is not the gift.
(It's so easy to make that mistake!)
It's what's inside that really counts!
The person is the gift!

I am a person, and therefore I am a gift—
  a gift to myself.
   a gift to God.
    a gift to others.
     a gift to the church.
      a gift to the world.

Sometimes I see my wrapping in the mirror.
And I may not like what I see.
And sometimes I wonder why I have a hard time
  loving and accepting the gift of me that God has given.
But if God loves me, then surely I must be lovable.

It seems that sometimes others are more
  concerned with my wrapping and don't even
    take the time to open the gift and look inside.
Sometimes I don't want them to,
  I want to be accepted, well liked.

Friendship in the church is about
  people who know that there's more
   to a person than their wrapping.
The people of the church are learning to
    see themselves and others
      as Jesus sees them,
       gifts from God,
        gifts to each other.

If I hold back the gift of my life, I lose it.
   That's what Jesus said.
But if I give my life to God and others,
    I will find it.
      That's what Jesus said.

I am a gift to the church,
   because I know that I am loved for more
      than my wrapping—more than my mirror image.
I am loved by God! From the inside out!
   That's what frees me to love myself
     and others in new ways.
   That's what helps me to be the church!

The room was quiet as Pastor Maria laid her poem down on her desk. Pastor David said, "It's a beautiful poem, Maria. I think it would be a good time for us to pray together."

Everyone was thoughtful as the pastor began: "Dear God, thank you for Maria's gift of a poem. And thank you for creating each of us to be so special and beautiful. You're the One who has given each of us our unique personalities, qualities, and talents. Help us to be willing to share what we are to help your church become everything it needs to be. And help us to love and accept one another in our church in the same way you love and accept us, just as we are. Amen."

Pastor David began to hand out scissors for the next activity as he said, "And now we want to take some time to build a church. Find Activity #6, 'The Church' and remove the page from your book."

activity

The children began cutting out the "church" as Pastor David continued. "This mountain looks a lot like the Mountain of Promise we created to represent ourselves, doesn't it? But did you notice the difference?"

Everyone responded by saying, "Jesus Christ."

"Of course. The church is built on the foundation of Jesus Christ. Let's take time away from our cutting to open our Bibles to Ephesians 2:19–22."

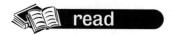

read

After reading the Scripture the class discussed it. "What does it mean to say that Jesus is the foundation of the church?"

discussion

Tyrel said, "Well, first of all, I think it means that the church wouldn't be here without Jesus Christ and people to believe in him. He's the one who started the church."

Pastor Maria added, "That's for sure, Tyrel. And it's true that in the same way that we as individuals are trying to build our lives on the teachings of Jesus Christ, that's what we're trying to do as a church, too. In fact, the church is made up of individuals who are all trying to do the same thing, and by now, you all know what that is, don't you?"

"Follow Jesus!" Joy said.

"Exactly!" Pastor Maria said. "We're trying to base everything we do as a church on the teachings of Jesus. We want to be guided by the Spirit of Jesus. Each side of this mountain represents one way we can do that. Take a colored marker and fill in one side with the word *worship*."

 activity

"What is worship?" Pastor Maria asked, as they wrote the word.

"It's singing!"

"And preaching!"

"And praying."

"It's giving an offering."

"It's giving praise and glory to God."

"It's showing God how much we love God."

"Yes, yes! It's all of those things," Pastor Maria continued. "The word worship really means 'worth-ship.' When we worship, we try to show God just how much God is worth to us. Everything we do in worship is for God. We don't go to worship to be entertained. We're there to serve God with our songs, prayers, offerings, praise, and love. That's why we call it a 'worship service.'"

"And another thing," Pastor David added. "We worship God with all of our hearts, minds, souls, and bodies. That means we worship God with everything we've got. So when we sing, we sing with all our heart. When we pray, we pray with all our soul. When we listen to the Word of God and the sermon, we listen with both of our ears and all our mind. In all these ways we try to show God how much we love and respect God."

Pastor Maria added, "So when we become members of our church, we promise to make worship a major priority! Do you think you can make that promise?"

The group agreed that they would try.

"Now, use a different color and write the word *education*," Pastor David said.

 activity

"Education isn't just about going to school. It's about learning whatever we can about life. So Christian education is all about learning about being a Christian. This class is a part of education, because we're learning to be followers of Jesus. A part of the promise we make to the church is to be involved throughout our life in learning more and more about the Bible and how we can be better Christians. That's why attending Sunday school and reading the Bible need to be a part of the promise. Don't forget that the word *disciple* means 'learner' or 'student.' To be a disciple of Jesus is to be his student."

Pastor Maria added, "Just as with worship, we need to learn with all of our hearts, minds, souls, and bodies. That means we need to get involved in learning and be hungry to know more and more about Jesus Christ. We need to pay attention to our teachers in order to learn all we can. Do you think you can promise that you will try hard to learn all you can about Jesus?"

The members of the class said, "We'll try!"

Pastor Maria continued, "Now write the word *fellowship* with another color."

 **activity**

"What is fellowship?"

Tyrel said, "I think it's a lot like what we have here in this class—friendship with others in the church, learning together, eating together, especially eating together." The class laughed because it had been Tyrel who had eaten the extra ice cream bar!

Pastor Maria said, "It's so important for us to have good Christian friends as we continue to grow in our relationship with God. I'm sure I wouldn't be a pastor today if I had not had so many wonderful friends to encourage me. Christian friends can really make a big difference. They teach us how to love others, not for the beautiful wrapping on the outside, but because we're loved by God and are learning to love each other for who we are on the inside, too."

"By the way, David and I have really grown to love all of you in the last few weeks, and that's what fellowship is all about—loving others with our hearts, minds, souls, and bodies. How many of you are willing to make a promise to try to love and accept everyone else in the church?"

The children all raised their hands.

"Would anyone like to guess what the last word is?" Pastor David paused.

"Giving money?" Joy suggested.

"Listening to the sermon?" Daniel smiled.

"Helping out?" Tyrel said, and when he did, Pastor David said, "That's pretty close. Who are we helping out?"

"The pastors?" Esteban smiled.

"Jesus?" Angela added.

"God?" Tyrel said.

"You're on the right track. We want to help God. Helping God is what we call the mission of the church. So write the word *mission* on the last side."

 **activity**

"We're to serve God, one another, and our world with all of our hearts, minds, souls, and bodies. That means that we need to be willing to do whatever God asks us to do. Are you all willing to promise that you will be involved in Jesus Christ's mission?"

They all nodded their heads that they would try.

 activity

As the children folded and taped their churches, Pastor Maria said, "There's a hymn we sometimes sing that says 'The church's one foundation is Jesus Christ her Lord.' And there's a verse in 1 Peter 5:10 that says Christ 'will himself perfect you and give you firmness, strength, and a sure foundation.' Our worship, fellowship, education, and mission all need to be based on Jesus Christ."

"I couldn't agree more," Pastor David said as he collected the scissors and markers. "Maria and I have committed and promised our lives to help the church be everything Jesus wants it to be. There are a lot of other careers we could have pursued, and I know we could be making a lot more money than we are, but we wouldn't be as rich in the things that matter. Maria and I have received so much more from God and the church than we'll ever be able to repay."

"David and I want to invite all of you to be open to God's calling," Pastor Maria added, "and not just to be baptized and follow Jesus. Be open to the call of God to pursue a full-time vocation serving Jesus Christ's church. We can highly recommend it as a wonderful career."

Their careers seemed far off in the future, but the children were interested to know that they could work in God's ministry, just like their new pastors. They'd never really considered it.

Pastor Maria opened her Bible and said, "Now let's open our Bibles to read the story of Jesus in Mark 14:22–42."

The members of the class took turns reading the verses and then filled in the blanks before they discussed the story.

 read   activity

Scripture for Today: Read Mark 14:22–42

Jesus said the bread was a symbol of what? _____

_____

_____

_____

He said the wine was a symbol of what? _____

_____

_____

_____

I think Jesus needed to pray to God because _____

_____

_____

_____

_____

I think some of the people may have wanted to arrest and kill Jesus because _____

_____

_____

_____

_____

discussion

Pastor Maria began the drum roll as she announced dramatically, "The BIG WORD for today is MISSION. Let me ask all of you, what was Jesus' main purpose for living? What was his mission in the world?"

discussion

Angela responded, "To start the church?"

And Daniel said, "To show us what God is like?"

Joy added, "To teach us how to love God and love each other?"

"Those are all excellent answers," Pastor Maria said. "If his mission in life was to love God and others with his whole life, what do you think our mission is? What is our purpose? Why did God create us? Our mission is the same as the mission of Jesus—to love God and others with our hearts, minds, souls, and bodies. Let's look up the word *mission* in the dictionary." The children wrote as Pastor Maria read slowly. Next, the children filled in the sentence completion exercise under the BIG WORD.

activity

The Big Word: MISSION

Dictionary definition: _____

_____

_____

_____

For Jesus the most important thing (the one thing he taught, lived, and died for—his mission) was _____

_____

_____

_____

_____

Saying that I am committed to the cause and mission of Jesus Christ in this world means that I'm willing to _____

_____

_____

_____

discussion

After their discussion, Pastor David invited the class members to write their prayers.

activity

My Prayer for Today

Thank you, God, that Jesus risked his life for the mission you gave him in this world. Right now, I'd say my mission or purpose in life is to _____

_____

_____

_____

_____

As I continue to grow into adulthood, help me to be willing to _____

_____

_____

Today I'm thankful for many things, including _____

_____

_____

_____

Forgive me for the time I _____

_____

_____

_____

Amen.

Those who were willing read their prayers while the class listened, and then Pastor Maria suggested a group hug. There were smiles of joy as they held one another close. A feeling growing inside each of the children told them that they were a part of something much bigger than themselves. They were standing not just on the floor of Pastor Maria's office but on a firm foundation, the love of Jesus Christ. They were standing in the fellowship of other believers, alive with the excitement of knowing that they were the church.

DAY 2: WEEK 5 ● MON ● TUE ● WED ● THU ● FRI ● SAT ● SUN (Check One)

Scripture for Today: Read Mark 14:43–65

If I had been one of the disciples when Jesus was arrested, I would have felt _____

_____

_____

_____

The question the high priest asked *(v. 61)* was _____

_____

_____

_____

Jesus answered by saying _____

_____

_____

_____

If I had been treated as Jesus was treated, I would have _____

_____

_____

_____

The Big Word: GIFTS

Dictionary definition: _____
_____
_____
_____

If someone is a very gifted person, it means that he or she _____
_____
_____
_____

Since God has given gifts to every person, I know that I am gifted, too. Some of my gifts, talents, and abilities are _____
_____
_____
_____

According to Ephesians 4:11–12, the reason God gave these gifts to me is so that I can
_____
_____
_____

My Prayer for Today

Dear Lord, thank you that you have given me a variety of gifts. Help me to know how I can use my gifts in your mission and for your purpose. A gift I have that could make our church a better church is _____
_____
_____
_____

I will offer this gift to you and the church by _____
_____
_____
_____

Thank you for the way Jesus used his gifts to show love to the world. I want to give you and the church the gift of my heart, mind, body, and soul. Please help me. Amen.

DAY 3: WEEK 5 | ○ MON ○ TUE ○ WED ○ THU ○ FRI ○ SAT ○ SUN | (Check One)

Scripture for Today: Read Mark 14:66–15:15

Peter denied that he knew Jesus. I sometimes don't tell others about Jesus because I'm afraid they might _____

_____

_____

_____

_____

_____

Peter denied that he knew Jesus. If my best friend did that to me, I'd feel _____

_____

_____

_____

_____

The crowd shouted, "Crucify him!" *(v. 13).* When I feel peer pressure to do what is wrong, I usually _____

_____

_____

_____

_____

The Big Word: SACRIFICE

Dictionary definition: _____

_____

_____

_____

If I sacrifice something for someone else it means that I _____

_____

_____

_____

_____

One person who has made sacrifices for me is (*How? What?*) _____
_____
_____
_____
_____
_____

According to Romans 12:1–2, what are we to sacrifice to God? _____
_____
_____
_____

I think Jesus was willing to sacrifice his life because _____
_____
_____
_____
_____

My Prayer for Today

Dear God, thank you for the sacrifice Jesus made on the cross for me. Help me to understand why _____
_____
_____
_____
_____

Forgive me for the times I'm not willing to _____
_____
_____
_____
_____

Help me to be willing to sacrifice my _____
_____
_____
_____
_____

Amen.

DAY 4: WEEK 5 ⬤ MON ⬤ TUE ⬤ WED ⬤ THU ⬤ FRI ⬤ SAT ⬤ SUN (Check One)

Scripture for Today: Read Mark 15:16–41

I believe that Jesus needed to die on the cross so that _____
_____
_____
_____
_____

One of the reasons others wanted him dead was that he _____
_____
_____
_____

Read verse 39. The Roman soldier said what he said because he believed _____
_____
_____
_____

The Big Word: CROSS

Dictionary definition: _____
_____
_____
_____

Some Christians choose to wear a cross around their neck as a reminder that they are
_____
_____
_____

If I wore a cross it would be because I believe that _____
_____
_____
_____

According to Mark 8:34, Jesus expects us to _____
_____
_____
_____

which means that we need to be willing to _____
_____
_____
_____

One question I have about the death of Jesus on the cross is _____
_____
_____
_____
_____
_____
_____
_____

My Prayer for Today

Dear God, Jesus said there is no greater love we can show for our friends than to die for them. Thank you that Jesus was willing to love me enough to die for me, to give his body, mind, heart, and soul so that I might find eternal life. Help me to understand why
_____
_____
_____
_____

Forgive me for _____
_____
_____
_____

Help me to be more willing to _____
_____
_____
_____

In Jesus' name, Amen.

DAY 5: WEEK 5 | ● MON ● TUE ● WED ● THU ● FRI ● SAT ● SUN | (Check One)

Scripture for Today: Read Mark 15:42–47

If I had been one of the women who knew and loved Jesus, when he died, I would have wanted to _____

_____

_____

_____

They showed their devotion and love for Jesus by _____

_____

_____

_____

I can show my devotion and love for Jesus by _____

_____

_____

_____

_____

The Big Word: FORGIVE

Dictionary definition: _____

_____

_____

_____

On the cross Jesus said, "Father, forgive them, for they don't know what they are doing." I think Jesus was willing to forgive others because _____

_____

_____

_____

He thought it was important to forgive others because if we don't, then we will _____

_____

_____

_____

Someone I need to forgive (or did forgive) is _____

_____

_____

_____

What for? _____

_____

_____

_____

_____

_____

_____

According to 1 John 1:9, God will forgive all of us our sins if we confess or admit our sins. I think that means that when God forgives me _____

_____

_____

_____

_____

My Prayer for Today

Dear God, please forgive me for _____

_____

_____

_____

_____

Help me to forgive others whenever they _____

_____

_____

_____

Thank you for accepting and loving me, even though I _____

_____

_____

_____

I pray that you will help me especially in my relationship with _____

_____

_____

_____

to be able to _____

_____

_____

_____

In Jesus' name, Amen.

DAY 6: WEEK 5 ● MON ● TUE ● WED ● THU ● FRI ● SAT ● SUN (Check One)

Scripture for Today: Read Mark 16:1–13

If someone asked me, "Do you really believe that Jesus Christ was raised from the dead?" I'd tell him or her _____

_____

_____

_____

because _____

_____

_____

_____

If Jesus were standing here with me right now, this is what I would want to say to him:

_____

_____

_____

_____

I'd want to ask him _____

_____

_____

_____

The Big Word: RESURRECTION

Dictionary definition: _____
_____
_____
_____

We celebrate the resurrection of Jesus on Easter Sunday. I think the reason that it's such an important day for the church is that _____
_____
_____
_____
_____
_____
_____

If Jesus could come back to life, that means that it's possible for me to live with God forever, too. Someday, I hope to be able to understand why _____
_____
_____
_____

In John 20:26–29 Jesus tells us that even though we can't see him, we can believe in him. If we do believe, we will _____
_____
_____
_____
_____

My Prayer for Today

Dear God, thank you for Easter! Thank you that Jesus came back to life and lives with us today. Help me on Easter and on every Sunday to remember that _____
_____
_____
_____

It's a challenge for me to _____
_____
_____
_____

So help me always to remember that _____
_____
_____
_____

Thank you for _____
_____
_____
_____

In the name of our resurrected Lord and Savior, Amen.

DAY 7: WEEK 5 ● MON ● TUE ● WED ● THU ● FRI ● SAT ● SUN (Check One)

Scripture for Today: Read Mark 16:14–20

Thinking about Jesus' statement "Whoever believes and is baptized will be saved" *(v. 16)* makes me want to _____
_____
_____
_____

One thing that helps me to believe in Jesus Christ and want to follow him is _____
_____
_____
_____

Reading the book of Mark has helped me to understand _____
_____
_____
_____

If Jesus asked me to give him my heart, mind, soul, and body, I'd tell him _____
_____
_____
_____

The Big Word: LIFE

Dictionary definition: _____
_____
_____
_____

I believe my life and all life comes from _____
_____
_____
_____

According to John 10:10, the reason Jesus came to this world was to give all of us _____
_____
_____
_____

I think this means that Jesus wants me to _____
_____
_____
_____

Jesus gave his life for us. If I give my life for him, it will mean that I will have to be willing to _____
_____
_____
_____
_____
_____

My Prayer for Today

Dear God, thank you for the gift of life. Help me to live my life for you. As I think about making a promise to give my heart, mind, soul, and body to you and your mission in this world, help me to _____
_____
_____
_____

Some things I still don't understand are _____
_____
_____
_____
_____
_____
_____
_____

As I think about the future and about living my life for Jesus Christ, I'm looking forward to _____
_____
_____
_____
_____
_____
_____
_____

I know I'll need your help, dear God. So help me always to _____
_____
_____
_____

In Jesus' name, Amen.

Declaration of Promise

CHAPTER 6

AN INVITATION TO

_____

TO BE BAPTIZED AND RECEIVE COMMUNION

DAY 1: WEEK 6  ● MON ● TUE ● WED ● THU ● FRI ● SAT ● SUN (Check One)

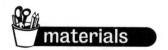

Copies of _Bridges of Promise_, Bibles, and pencils. You may also want to provide fresh bread and jam for the snack along with grape juice for the drink. Review Activity #7, "My Declaration of Promise to God."

THE STORY: FROM DEATH TO LIFE

By now the children wondered two things each time they arrived for class: "Where will we meet, and what will we eat?"

Once again their pastors had prepared a surprise. When the children came through the front doors of the church, Pastor Maria was standing behind a table cutting a fresh loaf of bread. The children began fixing their own sandwiches using the jars of peanut butter and jelly that were on the table, while Pastor Maria filled paper cups with grape juice.

"Where's Pastor David?" they asked.

"We'll find him in the sanctuary. As soon as we're finished here, let's go see what he's up to."

Pastor Maria escorted the group through the large doors into the sanctuary, down the center aisle to the front where Pastor David stood with a warm smile waiting at the Communion table. As Pastor Maria joined him behind the massive wooden table, the children settled in the front row of chairs.

"Welcome, my good friends!" Pastor David began. "Maria and I are glad you're here for this very important discussion about baptism and Communion. Write your names in the title for chapter 6, 'An Invitation to _____ to Be Baptized and Receive Communion.'"

Pastor Maria continued, "David and I thought this would be the best place to talk about the two ordinances of our church, because this is where we practice them on a regular basis. Does anyone know what the word *ordinance* means?"

discussion

Daniel's dad served on the police force, so he knew about city and traffic ordinances. "They're like laws or rules people have to obey."

"Right!" Pastor Maria said. "The word starts the same as 'order.' An 'order-ance' is an order to do, or not do, something. Did you know that Jesus gave us two ordinances? One is that we are to be baptized, and the other is that we are to take part in Communion."

Pastor David said, "In the daily assignments, you've now had a chance to read the whole story of Jesus in the book of Mark, so you know that before he was crucified on the cross, Jesus had his Last Supper with the disciples. And after he broke the bread, he told them to 'do this to remember me.' That's why we have Communion."

Pastor David and Maria stood side-by-side behind the Communion table, right where they always stood on the first Sunday of each month. Pastor Maria opened her Bible to 1 Corinthians 11:23–25 and began reading, "For I received from the Lord the teaching that I passed on to you: that the Lord Jesus, on the night he was betrayed, took a piece of bread…"

Pastor David picked up the loaf of bread and held it up as she continued to read, "…gave thanks to God, broke it, and said, 'This is my body, which is for you. Do this in memory of me.'"

Pastor David broke the bread in half, held up both pieces, and said, "Every time we break this bread, we're reminded of the broken body of our Lord. When we eat a piece of this bread, we're asked to remember the love of Jesus expressed to us when he gave his body on the cross. As the bread is being passed and we hold it in our hands, it's a good idea for us to pray to God and confess our sins and failures. Remember, if we confess our sins, God will forgive us."

Pastor Maria continued to read, "In the same way, after the supper he took the cup and said, 'This cup is God's new covenant, sealed with my blood. Whenever you drink it, do so in memory of me.'"

Pastor David held up the little glass of grape juice and said, "We're asked to remember the blood that Jesus shed for all of us, so that our sins might be forgiven. When the grape juice is being passed, think about God's love and renew your promise to love and serve Jesus Christ."

Pastor Maria added, "When you came in today, you ate peanut-butter-and-jam sandwiches. The food we eat nourishes every cell in our bodies. We couldn't live without food. In a similar way, when we eat this bread and drink this juice at Communion, our spiritual lives are being nourished. In a way, Jesus is becoming more and more a part of who we are. It's like spiritual food to help us keep our faith in Jesus alive. Be sure to remember Jesus and renew your promise to live your life for him."

"And remember, also," Pastor David added, "that there is nothing you have done or ever will do that will keep God from loving you. Always remember that. Communion reminds us that we are always being asked to come back to the table of God's love, no matter what we've done!"

Pastor Maria had disappeared through the door behind the platform area at the front of the sanctuary. All of a sudden, the curtains to the baptistry opened, and there stood Pastor Maria grinning inside the baptistry tank. "And now if I could have your attention over here, David and I want to invite you to step into the baptistry."

The children followed Pastor David through the door and down the steps into the tank. It was an eerie feeling to be standing in the dry tank looking out on the empty sanctuary.

Pastor David opened the Bible to the story of the baptism of Jesus in Mark 1:9–11.

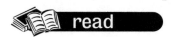 read

When Pastor David finished reading the story, he asked, "Why do you think Jesus wanted to be baptized?"

discussion

Joy said, "I always thought he wanted to show people how to do it!" It sounded logical.

"True," Pastor David said. "In fact, the way Matthew tells the same story (3:15), Jesus wanted to do all that God required of him. I think Jesus was baptized because he knew God wanted him to be baptized. We follow his example."

Pastor David thumbed through his Bible for another passage, and as he was looking, he asked, "Have you heard of baptizing babies by sprinkling or pouring water on their heads?" The children nodded. "Why do you suppose our church has decided that it's best to wait until children are older?"

discussion

Tyrel said, "It seems to me that there's no way babies can know what they're doing. It's not their own choice."

"That's right. We want children to be old enough to make their own choice, because that's what we believe the Bible teaches. When older children, youth, or adults have decided for themselves that they are ready to promise that they will follow Jesus as their Lord and Savior, it's time for them to be baptized."

Angela added, "I think that's good, because it's important that we know what we're doing and why we're doing it, before we do it!"

"Well put, Angela," Pastor David said. "In fact, that's why this class is so important. It gives you time to learn about Jesus, read and study the Bible, and think about it before you decide to be baptized."

Pastor Maria opened her Bible and read Colossians 2:12, "For when you were baptized, you were buried with Christ, and in baptism you were also raised with Christ through your faith in the active power of God, who raised him from death."

"May I have a volunteer to help me demonstrate what this verse means?" Daniel stepped forward, and Pastor Maria put her arm around his shoulders. She said, "When I baptize Daniel, I'll ask him two very important questions. First I'll ask, 'Daniel, do you believe that Jesus Christ is the Son of God?' and he'll say, 'Yes!' Then I'll ask him, 'And do you promise to the best of your ability, to follow and obey Jesus as one of his disciples as long as you live?' And Daniel will say, 'Yes!' Then I will baptize him."

Pastor Maria supported Daniel as she lowered him backward, immersing him all the way under the imaginary water. She asked Daniel, "What would happen if I held you under for a long time?"

"I'd drown!" Daniel choked. "But you wouldn't do that, would you?"

"Of course not," Pastor Maria smiled. "But that's why baptism is such a powerful symbol of death. Because staying under the water means physical death for us, just as staying under the influence of sin means spiritual death for us. But when we believe in Jesus, that's not what happens. The Bible says, 'We are raised with Christ...'" Pastor Maria began to lift Daniel as though bringing him up and out of the water. "It's the power of God that raises us from the power of death. What's the first thing people do when they come up out of the water?"

"Breathe!" Daniel declared, relieved. "That's what I'd do."

"Right, Daniel. In fact, they take a deep breath of air. To me, it's a lot like breathing in the Spirit of God. We can't see God, but we know God's Spirit, or presence, is everywhere, so when we breathe God's Spirit into our lives, we are actually taking in the gift of eternal life."

Pastor David said, "Let's go back to our chairs now, because it's time to think about some of the promises you want to make to God. Find Activity #7, 'My Declaration of Promise to God' on page 153."

The children returned to their seats and removed the activity page. Pastor David continued, "We've come to a very important time in the process of learning about being disciples of Jesus. Some of you may have already decided to promise to live your whole lives for him. Others may not be sure, quite yet. That's okay. Pastor Maria and I want all of you to think seriously about each of the statements on this declaration sheet and decide 'yes,' 'no,' or 'not yet' for each one. It's very important that you be honest with yourself and with God. In a moment I'll have you scatter around the sanctuary. You can find a place on the floor or in a chair, and then, prayerfully, fill out your own declaration of promise. Pastor Maria and I will wait here at the front if you have any questions or want to talk privately about any of this. When you've filled out the page, bring your sheet to one of us to share what you have decided."

With paper and pencil in hand, the children scattered around the sanctuary, and for a few minutes, all was quiet as each child thought and prayed about the promises they wanted to make to God. Pastor David and Maria prayerfully waited. When each of the children had finished completing their "Declaration of Promise," their pastors affirmed them and listened as they expressed their decisions and choices.

When all had settled back in their chairs, Pastor Maria said, "David and I are so excited about all that you've been learning. We're so pleased to know that many of you have already decided to be followers of Jesus and be baptized. For those of you who have not yet made that decision, that's okay. Remember that all of you need to make sure that the time is right for you. And, of course, David and I are praying that, when you're ready, you'll let us know."

"And now it's time to read the 'Scripture for Today.' We're going to read the account of Jesus' baptism in Matthew." The children took turns reading the verses, and after completing the sentences, they discussed the baptism story in Matthew.

Scripture for Today: Read Matthew 3:13–17

According to Matthew, Jesus decided to be baptized because he believed _____

_____

_____

_____

_____

_____

_____

If and when I decide to be baptized it will be because I believe _____

_____

_____

_____

_____

I think baptism helped Jesus to _____

_____

_____

_____

Baptism will help me to _____

_____

_____

_____

Pastor Maria smiled as she began the familiar drum roll. "Can anyone guess what the BIG WORD for today might be?" "Baptize!" the children yelled together. "Exactly. Today's BIG WORD is BAPTIZE. We've already talked a little about what that word means to us as Baptists. Let's see what the dictionary has to say about it." The children listened and carefully wrote Webster's definition as Pastor Maria read it aloud. Then they did the sentence completion exercise.

activity

The Big Word: BAPTIZE

Dictionary definition: _____

_____

_____

_____

The Greek word for baptism in the Bible means "to go all the way under the water," or be immersed. One question I have about baptism is _____

_____

_____

_____

A person is ready to be baptized if he or she _____

_____

After the children shared their thoughts about the BIG WORD, Pastor David said, "Okay, now I'd like to tell you about some of the first Baptists, the people who got the Baptist church started."

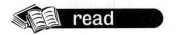

Famous Baptists: John Smyth

John Smyth was a person who spoke his mind. In 1602 he was a preacher in England at the Anglican Cathedral of Lincoln. He wasn't afraid to tell the people in his congregation that he didn't agree with the system of priests and bishops. He believed the only real foundation for the church was what was in the Bible, not church tradition. He lost his job, but soon found a new position with a group of Separatists in Gainsborough, England. Separatists were believers who wanted to separate from the Church of England. The group was persecuted, so they decided to move to Holland in 1606.

John Smyth studied his Bible and concluded that the early church was made up only of those who had accepted Jesus Christ as Lord and Savior. He also concluded that only those who had done this were to be baptized.

In 1609 Smyth and thirty-six members of his congregation declared that their infant baptisms were not valid. Smyth first baptized himself, then the rest of the congregation. Together they became the first Baptist church ever.

In America, the story of Baptists begins with Roger Williams, a minister of the Church of England who wanted freedom in America. He began the colony of Rhode Island, and in 1638 started the First Baptist Church in Providence, Rhode Island.

Baptists grew rapidly from ten thousand in 1775 to one hundred thousand in 1800. In 1900 they numbered over five million, and today are the largest Protestant group in North America with millions of members in several different Baptist denominations or groups all over the world.

 discussion

Discuss the material above.

"I think it is important to know about our history and about how our church came to be," Pastor Maria concluded. "Baptism was important to John Smyth and Roger Williams, so important that they started a new church and a new colony. Keep that in mind as you write your prayers now and talk to God about baptism."

 activity

My Prayer for Today

Thank you, God, that Jesus was baptized and has invited me to be baptized, too. Help me to understand why _____

_____

_____

_____

_____

Thank you for the courage John Smyth had. Help me to have the courage to _____

_____

_____

_____

_____

Today I'm especially thankful for _____

_____

_____

_____

_____

Amen.

Pastors David and Maria invited the children to stand in a circle at the front of the sanctuary while different members of the class volunteered to read their prayers. Finally, Pastor David closed with this prayer:

"Dear God, this has been a wonderful day to think about the bread and juice and your love for us in Jesus Christ. Thank you also for the water of baptism and for the gift of new life that baptism shows us. Thanks most of all for each of these good friends of mine and the promises they have made to you. Guide them every day of their lives as they follow you as their Lord and Savior. In Jesus' name, Amen."

DAY 2: WEEK 6 ● MON ● TUE ● WED ● THU ● FRI ● SAT ● SUN (Check One)

Scripture for Today: Read Luke 22:14–27

When Jesus said, "This is my body which is given for you," I think he was saying that the bread is a symbol of _____
_____
_____
_____

When Jesus said, "This is my blood," I think he meant that the grape juice is a symbol of
_____
_____
_____

If Jesus expects me to be one who "serves" *(v. 27)*, then I need to find ways to _____
_____
_____
_____

The Big Word: COMMUNION

Dictionary definition: _____
_____
_____
_____

If the word *communion* means "with union," some of the things in my life that keep me from feeling close to God are _____
_____
_____
_____

Those things that help me feel close to or in union with God are _____

_____

_____

_____

Famous Baptists: The Judsons

One very hot summer in 1806, a group of students ran for a haystack to get out of a thunderstorm. While the storm raged, Adoniram Judson talked with his friends about a day in the future when he would, hopefully, become a missionary to Asia. It had been a dream of his for a long while.

(Note: Begin asking God to help you dream of ways you can serve God now and in the future.)

A few years after that thunderstorm, these same young men organized the first American missionary organization sponsored by the Congregational churches.

Adoniram and his wife Ann were the first to go. They boarded a ship in 1812. Their goal was India. During the long voyage, they had plenty of time to study the Bible and pray. They made a startling discovery as they read their Bibles. They could find no place in the Bible that talked about baptizing babies. As they continued their search of the New Testament, they concluded that baptism is intended only for those who personally believe in Jesus as their Lord and Savior.

One of the first things they did when they got off the boat in India was to be immersed in water in the same way that Jesus was baptized in the Jordan River.

Encouraged by the government of India to move on to a different place, Adoniram and Ann were pioneer missionaries to Burma (modern-day Myanmar) where today millions of Baptists worship God and baptize thousands of new believers every year. The work of the Judsons set an example for others to go as missionaries to other parts of the world, and today, there are thousands of missionaries serving Christ all over the world.

You will find Ann and Adoniram's last name on this book, since Judson Press, our Baptist publishing house, is named in their honor.

My Prayer for Today

Dear Lord, thank you for people like the Judsons who gave their lives to serve you. Thank you that they had the courage to be baptized. Help me as I prepare to be baptized to _____

_____

_____

_____

And whenever I take Communion, help me always to remember that _____

_____

_____

_____

Thank you for Jesus, my Lord and Savior. Forgive me for the times that I _____

_____

_____

_____

I praise you for _____

_____

_____

_____

Amen.

DAY 3: WEEK 6 ● MON ● TUE ● WED ● THU ● FRI ● SAT ● SUN (Check One)

Scripture for Today: Read Matthew 25:31–46

Some of the ways Jesus expects us to serve those in need include _____

_____

_____

_____

_____

_____

_____

The sheep represent people who _____
_____
_____
_____

The goats represent people who _____
_____
_____
_____

When I'm old, I hope Jesus will be able to say to me, "Well done, _____,
you have been faithful to me by _____
_____
_____
_____
_____

The Big Word: FAITHFUL

Dictionary definition: _____
_____
_____
_____

If I am faithful to my schoolwork, it means that teachers can count on me to _____
_____
_____
_____

If I say I am faithful to Jesus Christ, it means that Jesus can count on me to _____
_____
_____
_____

I'm being faithful to God when I _____
_____
_____
_____
_____

Famous Baptists: Walter Rauschenbusch

In the 1800s and early 1900s the population in the United States grew rapidly, with many immigrants coming from other countries. Walter Rauschenbusch (1861–1918), a German Baptist minister, cared for the suffering people crowded into the big cities. He worked in a very challenging and poor area of New York City called "Hell's Kitchen."

He preached the gospel of Jesus and believed that the Good News of Jesus had a lot to say about how people should live and work. Rauschenbusch fought for shorter working hours (eight-hour days) and fewer working days (two-day weekends). He opposed the use and abuse of children as laborers in factories and mines, and he fought for better working conditions for women.

He is famous for preaching that Jesus wants to establish "the kingdom of God" in the hearts and lives of people. He is remembered in American history as one who helped to lead the way to a fairer, better life for common people, and he did it all because of his belief in Jesus.

My Prayer for Today

Dear God, thank you for people like Walter Rauschenbusch. Help me to be a person who is also willing to _____

_____

_____

_____

Thank you for the sacrifice Jesus made on the cross for me. Help me to be faithful to Jesus in the way I _____

_____

_____

Thanks for the many things I am learning about you, such as _____

_____

_____

Amen.

DAY 4: WEEK 6 ● MON ● TUE ● WED ● THU ● FRI ● SAT ● SUN (Check One)

Scripture for Today: Read Matthew 26:36–56

Jesus prayed to God asking that he might be relieved of the suffering that was ahead of him. I think Jesus must have felt _____

_____

_____

_____

The disciples had a hard time staying awake while Jesus was praying. I think Jesus must have felt _____

_____

_____

_____

I wonder why Jesus _____

_____

_____

_____

The Big Word: HOPE

Dictionary definition: _____

_____

_____

_____

Some day I hope to go *(where?)* _____

_____

_____

_____

Some day I hope to *(do what?)* _____

_____

_____

_____

Some day I want to become a person who _____

_____

_____

_____

_____

_____

I hope to be able to serve God by _____

_____

_____

_____

_____

_____

_____

Hebrews 11:1 says that hope is _____

_____

_____

_____

_____

_____

Famous Baptists: Lott Cary

Lott Cary was born into slavery and without much hope. In order to forget his miserable life, he began to drink liquor and became an alcoholic. At the age of twenty-seven, Cary became a believer in Christ and a member of the First Baptist Church of Richmond, Virginia. God helped him to change his life. He stopped drinking and began telling others about the power of Jesus Christ to change lives. He learned to read so that he could read the Bible. In time, he was able to buy his freedom for $850 (a large amount of money back then). Just two years later, he helped form the Richmond African Baptist Missionary Society. Cary was able to interest others in the idea of telling other Africans about Jesus, and in 1821 the Baptist General Convention chose Lott Cary as a missionary to Liberia, West Africa. Lott Cary is known as the first American missionary ever to go to Africa.

My Prayer for Today

Dear God, thank you for courageous people like Lott Cary. Thank you for his willingness to tell others about Jesus and about the hope he had in you. Give me a strong hope that you are able to _____

_____

_____

_____

_____

Give me the courage to tell others about Jesus, especially (list people you know who need to hear about Jesus) _____

_____

_____

_____

_____

Thank you for the many ways you have helped me to _____

_____

_____

_____

_____

_____

In Jesus' name, Amen.

DAY 5: WEEK 6 ● MON ● TUE ● WED ● THU ● FRI ● SAT ● SUN (Check One)

Scripture for Today: Read John 15:5–17

When Jesus said, "I am the vine, and you are the branches," I think he was telling me that in my relationship with Jesus I am _____

_____

_____

_____

_____

_____

To "remain" in Jesus as long as I live means that I _____
_____
_____
_____

If my life is to "bear much fruit (many good things)," I know I'll need to _____
_____
_____
_____
_____

Verse 9 tells us that if we are to love God, we also need to _____
_____
_____
_____

The Big Word: JOY

Dictionary definition: _____
_____
_____
_____

I have joy when I _____
_____
_____
_____
_____

I also have joy when someone else _____
_____
_____
_____

In John 15:11, Jesus tells that the reason that God sent him was to _____
_____
_____
_____

Famous Baptists: Helen Barrett Montgomery

Helen Barrett Montgomery was a woman ahead of her time (1861–1934). She spent her life working for the church and was the first woman to be elected to the Rochester, New York, school board. She taught Sunday school at the Lake Avenue Baptist Church, where she was a member. She helped to organize a dental clinic and an open-air school for children with tuberculosis, and she established the first factory school in the nation.

She became the first president of the Women's Educational and Industrial Union of Rochester, sponsored a legal aid center to help the poor, and helped to create the first public playground. This all was at a time when few women could take leadership roles.

In Baptist history, she is famous for being the first woman to be the national president of what is now the American Baptist Churches USA. In fact, she was the first woman president ever to head a major church denomination. In her spare time she translated the Greek New Testament into modern English and wrote a best-seller, *The King's Highway*.

My Prayer for Today

Dear God, thank you for people like Helen Barrett Montgomery who had the vision and determination to use the gifts you gave her to serve your church. As Helen Barrett Montgomery served, help me to be willing to _____
_____
_____
_____
_____
_____

Give me a vision for _____
_____
_____
_____
_____

Give me your gift of joy, especially when I am _____

_____

_____

_____

In Jesus' name, Amen.

DAY 6: WEEK 6 ● MON ● TUE ● WED ● THU ● FRI ● SAT ● SUN (Check One)

Scripture for Today: Read Matthew 5:1–12

If someone asked me, "Are you happy?" I'd say _____

_____

_____

_____

because _____

_____

_____

People try to find happiness in a lot of ways, including _____

_____

_____

_____

Five ways to happiness that Jesus offers in Matthew 5:1–12 include
1. _____
2. _____
3. _____
4. _____
5. _____

Jesus says in verse 9 that those who work for peace are blessed or happy. An example of working for peace in my family or with my friends is _____

_____

_____

_____

In verse 11, I think it's hard to understand _____
_____
_____
_____
_____

The Big Word: PEACE

Dictionary definition: _____
_____
_____
_____

The room in my house where I feel the most peace is _____
_____
_____
_____
_____

I feel peace often when I'm with _____
_____
_____
_____
_____

I don't feel peace when _____
_____
_____
_____
_____

Galations 5:22 lists peace as one of the fruits of the Spirit of God. If I'm to grow in my peacefulness, I will need God to help me _____
_____
_____
_____
_____
_____

Famous Baptists: Martin Luther King Jr.

Dr. Martin Luther King Jr. (1929–1968) was a Baptist who lived as a follower of Jesus Christ. He graduated from Morehouse College, Crozer Theological Seminary, and Boston University and served as pastor of the Dexter Street Baptist Church in Montgomery, Alabama, from 1954 to 1960.

He is best remembered for leading peaceful demonstrations for civil rights, like the Montgomery bus boycott. He was awarded the Nobel Peace Prize in 1964. King said, "Nonviolence is the answer to the crucial political and racial questions of our time."

An assassin's bullet took his life in Memphis, Tennessee, on April 4, 1968. He died for his conviction that all people are equal and should be treated fairly. He gave his life believing that Jesus' love must be made real by ending prejudice, violence, and injustice in our world.

My Prayer for Today

Dear God, thank you for Martin Luther King Jr., who was willing to give his life fighting for what is right. Help me to work for peace, especially in my relationship with

_____
_____
_____
_____

Forgive me whenever I think another person is less than I am because of his or her clothing, color of skin, or unattractiveness. Forgive me for thinking that _____

_____
_____
_____
_____

Thank you for accepting and loving me even though I _____

_____
_____

In Jesus' name, Amen.

DAY 7: WEEK 6 ⬤ MON ⬤ TUE ⬤ WED ⬤ THU ⬤ FRI ⬤ SAT ⬤ SUN (Check One)

Scripture for Today: Read Philippians 2:1–11

Some of the words in the passage that describe Jesus are _____
_____
_____
_____

To say that Jesus was humble means that he _____
_____
_____
_____

If I'm to have the "attitude...that Christ Jesus had," then I will need to spend more time
_____
_____
_____

The Big Word: HUMBLE

Dictionary definition: _____
_____
_____
_____

I show humility with my family when I _____
_____
_____
_____

I show humility with teachers at school when I _____
_____
_____

I show humility with friends when I _____
_____
_____

I show humility toward God when I _____

_____

_____

_____

_____

Famous Baptists: Charles Evans Hughes

Charles Evans Hughes served as the chief justice of the United States Supreme Court, yet he was also a humble follower of Jesus Christ.

Hughes served as the governor of New York from 1907 to 1910. He taught Sunday school at Fifth Avenue Baptist Church in New York City, which later became known as Riverside Church.

In 1910 he became the first president of the Northern Baptist Convention (later called American Baptist Churches of the USA).

He was the Republican candidate for president in 1916 and lost to Woodrow Wilson in one of the closest elections in United States history.

Hughes served as chief justice of the United States Supreme Court from 1930 to 1941. Historian Dexter Perkins wrote about him, "He was almost invariably on the side of freedom."

Because of his deep Christian convictions, Hughes believed in religious freedom. He worked for freedom of the press and for civil rights.

My Prayer for Today

Dear God, thank you for powerful people like Charles Evans Hughes, who realized that all of life and power come from you. Thank you that he used the gifts you gave him to serve the cause of freedom. In the same way that he was committed to Jesus Christ and lived for Jesus, I want to _____

_____

_____

_____

_____

Give me the gift of humility, especially when _____
_____
_____
_____
_____
_____

I am very thankful to you for many things, including _____
_____
_____
_____
_____
_____

In Jesus' name, Amen.

CHAPTER 7

_____

(Write your name here.)

IS A BRIDGE OF PROMISE TO OTHERS

DAY 1: WEEK 7 ● MON ● TUE ● WED ● THU ● FRI ● SAT ● SUN (Check One)

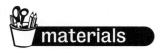
materials

Copies of _Bridges of Promise_, Bibles, and pencils. You may also want to have cookies and milk for a snack. Review Activity #8, "Bridges of Promise."

THE STORY: THE GOLDEN GATE

The children were surprised to discover a gallon of milk and a plate of warm cookies right at the front doors of the church where Pastors Maria and David met the children.

"Pastor David and I decided we wanted to meet right here at the front doors of the church," Pastor Maria said, "because it's the place where we enter the church building, but it's also the place where we go into the world after we've been with God in worship. And today we want to talk about some of the ways we can be like a bridge from God to the world."

"That's right," Pastor David added. "When we leave this place and the relationships we have here, we go to many places—our homes, neighborhoods, schools, workplaces—and when we go, God asks us to be bridges of promise to the world. Find chapter 7 in your book, '_____ Is a Bridge of Promise to Others,' and write your names in the title."

Pastor Maria handed each child a rolled-up tube of paper. As they pulled the rubber bands off and opened the gift, they discovered a poster inside.

Find Activity Sheet #8 in the back of your books.

"It's a bridge!" Tyrel said.

"It looks like the Golden Gate in San Francisco!" Angela said. "We were there just last summer!"

"You're right, Angela. It is the Golden Gate, and we want you to have this picture as a reminder of two things. First, always remember that Jesus is our bridge to God. It is through him that we come to know God's love and God's purpose for our lives."

"And second," Pastor David continued, "whenever you look at this picture, remember to see yourself as a bridge from God to other people. In other words, we are like this Golden Gate Bridge whenever others discover the love of God through us."

"Just think of it," Pastor Maria said. "If we are the body of Christ, we represent Christ in the world, and everywhere we go, we represent Jesus. You may be the only sermon some people will ever hear."

Esteban was studying the Golden Gate photo. "I guess I don't think of myself as a Golden Gate Bridge—more like a tiny log across a little stream."

The class laughed as Pastor David responded, "Even so, we all need to know that just as the Golden Gate is a very high and mighty bridge. God has high hopes for all of us that we will make a mighty difference in this world for God!"

Pastor Maria invited the children to turn in their Bibles to Luke 4:18–19. Joy read the words of Jesus: "The Spirit of the Lord is upon me, because he has chosen me to bring good news to the poor. He has sent me to proclaim liberty to the captives and recovery of sight to the blind, to set free the oppressed and announce that the time has come when the Lord will save his people."

"Read verse 21, also." Pastor Maria seemed intent on the importance of this verse.

Joy read, "He said to them, 'This passage of Scripture has come true today, as you heard it being read.'"

"I wonder why he said that." Maria was probing. "How do you think this Scripture came true in the life and ministry of Jesus? We've been reading the story of Jesus in Mark during the past few weeks," Pastor Maria continued. "What are some of the ways Jesus lived out this Scripture through ministering and serving? How was Jesus like God's bridge to others? And what are some of the ways you and I can be like Jesus in being a bridge of kindness, love, and service to others?"

 discussion

Talk about each of the above questions before going on.

Pastor David invited the class to find Activity #8 in their books and gave this instruction: "Think of ways you are like God's bridge to the places where you live—your home, school, church, and neighborhood. Write down at least one idea in each box, and then we'll discuss what you've come up with."

 activity    discussion

You'll find this activity on the back of the bridge photo.

"Whenever we represent the love and goodness of Jesus to our friends, neighbors, and family—even people we don't know or like—we are like bridges of promise to them," Pastor David said.

 activity

Optional Activity: If you have access to the Internet, click onto www.abc-usa.org to explore some of the headlines of what is happening in national and international ministries. Discuss with the children the importance of being a part of a worldwide network of people who are acting on our behalf as bridges of promise to the world. Discuss, also, the way your church supports the efforts of these "bridges of promise" through the offerings you receive for missions.

"And now it's time to read today's Scripture," said Pastor David. "Let's read it together." The children all turned in their Bibles to Philippians 1:1–11.

 activity

Scripture for Today: Read Philippians 1:1–11

Some of the things Paul says to express his love and friendship to his friends in the church in Philippi are _____

_____

_____

_____

I think Paul is thankful because _____

_____

_____

_____

I'm thankful to God for _____

_____

_____

_____

_____

Pastor Maria announced, "Time for the BIG WORD! Today's is THANKS. Let's see what the dictionary has to say about it before we complete the sentence exercise."

activity

The Big Word: THANKS

Dictionary definition: _____

_____

_____

_____

_____

It's important to tell others that we're thankful because _____

_____

_____

_____

_____

It's important to tell God that we're thankful because _____

_____

_____

_____

"It is important to say thank-you to God for all of the blessings we have been given," Pastor David said. "Let's take the time to do that now as we write our prayer for today. One thing I know I'm thankful for is this class—and I want to tell God how grateful I am for each one of you."

 activity

My Prayer for Today

Thank you, God, that this class has helped me to _____

_____

_____

_____

Thank you for the Bible and for helping me to understand that _____

_____

_____

_____

In the future help me to be more thankful for _____

_____

_____

_____

Amen.

 discussion

The children spent time thinking about the Bible passage, the BIG WORD, and writing their prayers. When they had completed the activity, Pastor Maria led in a discussion about thankfulness, and expressed how thankful she and David had become for each one of them.

"Next week we're going to meet for our final class at the same place we began. Do you remember that far back?"

How could the children forget the homemade pizza and fun they had had at their pastors' apartment? Remembering back, they were all very thankful for the new friendships that had been built and for all they had learned about being disciples of Jesus.

"We're planning to have a baptism service on Easter Sunday, so check your schedules. David and I are so excited about the way you have promised to live your lives for God and be baptized. You've all grown so much, and so have we! You're an amazing group!

We'll never forget this class and each one of you. And now, let's end our class today by forming a bridge at the entrance, and exit, of our church building."

They formed a line facing the doors of the church with each person's hands on the shoulders of the person in front of them. They looked sort of like a bridge, and even though they weren't the Golden Gate, there was something beautiful, strong, and graceful about their little bridge. Maybe they were the Golden Gate Bridge from the church to the world, after all.

As they stood looking very bridge-like, Pastor Maria said this prayer:

"Dear God, what a wonderful time we've had today thinking about how we can each, in our own way, make a positive difference in our families, schools, church, and world. I pray that the friendships we have started in this class and the love that we have for each other will spill over into the world as we leave this place. Help us to be your Golden Gate Bridges to the world! In the name of Jesus, the best bridge of all, Amen."

DAY 2: WEEK 7 ● MON ● TUE ● WED ● THU ● FRI ● SAT ● SUN (Check One)

Scripture for Today: Read Galatians 5:22–23

Some qualities (fruit) that show to others that God's Spirit is in my life are _____
_____
_____
_____
_____
_____

One of the qualities that I think is already present in my life is _____
_____
_____
_____
_____

One quality that I know I need God to help me develop is _____
_____
_____
_____
_____
_____

The Big Word: FRUITFUL

Dictionary definition: _____
_____
_____
_____

If I've had a "fruitful day at school," it means that I _____
_____
_____
_____

In order for my life to become more fruitful for God, I know I will need to _____
_____
_____
_____

My Prayer for Today

Dear Lord, thank you that you have given me the fruit of _____
_____
_____
_____

In all of my relationships with family and friends, help me to be more _____
_____
_____
_____

I want to be filled with your Spirit, so that people will be able to see that I _____
_____
_____
_____

Thank you for _____
_____
_____
_____

Amen.

DAY 3: WEEK 7 ● MON ● TUE ● WED ● THU ● FRI ● SAT ● SUN (Check One)

Scripture for Today: Read Romans 12:9–21

Name five things from this passage that are signs that we are faithful and devoted to God:

1. _____
2. _____
3. _____
4. _____
5. _____

Others: _____
_____
_____

The Big Word: DEVOTION

Dictionary definition: _____
_____
_____
_____

Serving God "with a heart full of devotion" *(Romans 12:11),* means that I will _____
_____
_____
_____

One way I'd like to serve God more is _____
_____
_____
_____

My Prayer for Today

Thank you for being willing to help me _____
_____
_____

I want to grow in my faith every day. Help me to take the time to _____
_____
_____
_____
_____

Amen.

DAY 4: WEEK 7 ⬤ MON ⬤ TUE ⬤ WED ⬤ THU ⬤ FRI ⬤ SAT ⬤ SUN (Check One)

Scripture for Today: Read Deuteronomy 14:22–23

If I tithe one tenth of $10.00 to God, it means that I would give God $_____.
(Move the decimal point one place to the left.)

If I received $1,000,000.00, a tithe would be how much? $_____. *(Move the decimal point one place to the left.)*

I think God wants us to tithe because it helps us to _____
_____
_____
_____
_____

And it helps God to _____
_____
_____
_____

The Big Word: TITHE

Dictionary definition: _____
_____
_____
_____

I think it's a good thing for me to tithe or give one tenth of the money that comes to me. In the future I will try to _____

_____

_____

_____

Some people might find it hard to tithe because they _____

_____

_____

_____

I want to promise God that in my giving to the church and to God's work in the world, I will always try to _____

_____

_____

_____

_____

My Prayer for Today

Dear God, help me to be generous with my love, time, service, and money as a way of saying thanks for all you have given to me. Forgive me for the times I _____

_____

_____

_____

In the future, please help me to be willing to _____

_____

_____

_____

I love you with all of my heart, mind, soul, and strength. Help me show my generosity in the way I _____

_____

_____

_____

_____

Amen.

DAY 5: WEEK 7 ● MON ● TUE ● WED ● THU ● FRI ● SAT ● SUN (Check One)

Scripture for Today: Read Matthew 9:9

If I had been Matthew, and Jesus had said to me, "Follow me!" I think I would have felt

_____

_____

_____

Matthew probably wanted to follow Jesus because he believed Jesus was _____

_____

_____

_____

Matthew probably invited Jesus to his home because he _____

_____

_____

The Big Word: FOLLOW

Dictionary definition: _____

_____

_____

_____

A leader is only a leader if there are those who are willing to follow. Some things about Jesus that make me want to follow him are _____

_____

_____

_____

I'm a leader for Jesus Christ whenever I _____

_____

_____

○ *I have not yet decided to follow Jesus.*

○ *I have decided to follow Jesus.*

My Prayer for Today

Dear God, thank you for people like Matthew who were willing to follow and obey you as Lord and Savior. In saying that I'm willing to follow you, I know I'll have to

_____
_____
_____
_____

Sometimes I don't want to _____

_____
_____
_____

Teach me how to _____

_____
_____
_____

Thank you for the people in my life who have taught me and led me to know more about Jesus, especially _____

_____
_____
_____

Amen.

DAY 6: WEEK 7 ● MON ● TUE ● WED ● THU ● FRI ● SAT ● SUN (Check One)

Scripture for Today: Read Colossians 3:12–17

What are some of the articles of "clothing" that a follower of Jesus Christ needs to put on every day? _____

_____
_____
_____
_____

Verse 17 gives a good guide or measure for living our lives as Christians. By what do we measure what we do and say? _____

_____

_____

_____

Why do we need to have thanksgiving in our hearts? *(v. 16)* _____

_____

_____

_____

The Big Word: CHOSEN

Dictionary definition: _____

_____

_____

_____

If I'm invited to a party or chosen to be a part of a team or group, it makes me feel

_____

_____

_____

To say that we have been chosen by God *(Colossians 3:12)* is to say that each one of us

_____

_____

_____

Knowing that God has chosen and loved me helps me to feel _____

_____

_____

_____

My life will show others that I have chosen to love and serve God if I _____

_____

_____

_____

_____

My Prayer for Today

Dear God, thank you for choosing me for your team. Teach me how to _____

_____

_____

_____

_____

_____

Help me have the courage to _____

_____

_____

_____

_____

Help others to see that I am _____

_____

_____

_____

_____

I praise and thank you for _____

_____

_____

_____

_____

Amen.

DAY 7: WEEK 7 ● MON ● TUE ● WED ● THU ● FRI ● SAT ● SUN (Check One)

Scripture for Today: Read Ephesians 2:4–10

Review: How is it that we are saved? _____

_____

_____

_____

_____

How did God show love for all of us? _____

_____

_____

_____

Why were we created? *(v.10)* _____

_____

_____

_____

_____

_____

The Big Word: MINISTER

Dictionary definition: _____

_____

_____

_____

If someone is in need of help, and I "minister" to him or her, it means that I _____

_____

_____

_____

For me to be a minister of Jesus Christ means that I am _____

_____

_____

_____

God calls us to "a life of good deeds" *(Ephesians 2:10)*. Some of the good things I've already done for God and others this week are _____

_____

_____

_____

I'm a minister whenever I _____

_____

_____

_____

My Prayer for Today

Dear God, help me think of myself as a minister. Help me always be ready to do good things for you and other people. Thank you for those who minister to me, including

_____
_____
_____
_____
_____

Help me find new ways to minister to _____

_____
_____
_____
_____

Forgive me for the times I _____

_____
_____
_____
_____

I praise and thank you today for _____

_____
_____
_____
_____

In Jesus' name, Amen.

CHAPTER 8

I, _____ ,

(Write your name here.)

AM GROWING IN MY FAITH

DAY 1: WEEK 8 ● MON ● TUE ● WED ● THU ● FRI ● SAT ● SUN (Check One)

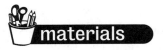

Copies of *Bridges of Promise*, Bibles, and pencils. Ice-cream sundaes make an excellent snack for today. Review Activity #9, "Good Nutrition."

THE STORY: FEEDING THE SOUL

The children arrived at Pastor David and Maria's apartment right on schedule. Pastor David escorted them directly into the kitchen where Pastor Maria explained the rules for a make-an-animal-with-your-sundae contest. With a variety of toppings, nuts, and whipped cream, they went to work creating their masterpieces. When they were finished, everyone agreed that Tyrel's zebra was the most fun and creative, that is, until he ate it.

"These past weeks have gone so fast," said Pastor David. "Maria and I have had a lot of fun with all of you. Thanks for being so faithful in your attendance. That's partly why we wanted to celebrate today with ice cream—to honor all of you for your accomplishment. We know it's been hard work, but you've done very well, and we're especially thankful for the promises you've made to God. We can hardly wait until Easter Sunday and the baptism!"

"Today we want to discuss with you some of the ways to keep faith alive," Pastor Maria started the lesson. "Find chapter 8 in your books and write your name in the title, 'I, _____, Am Growing in My Faith.' After you've done that, find Activity Sheet #9 entitled, 'Good Nutrition,' and take a look at the nutrition chart that's at the top of the page."

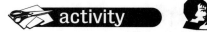

"Name some of the things you've eaten today and see if we can place each one on the food chart." The group discussed the importance of well-balanced diets. Some children were surprised that fruits, vegetables, and grains are the most important part of a good diet.

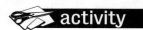

"And now," Pastor David continued, "Maria and I feel it's very important to discuss with you another kind of nutrition that's good for the soul. Let's see how many things we can think of that help us grow in our Christian faith. Each time one of us comes up with a new one, let's write it in the chart at the bottom of the page."

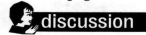

"I'd say *prayer* is pretty important," Esteban said.

"Yes, definitely, prayer," Pastor Maria said as the children wrote the word in one of the spaces on the chart. "And not just before bedtime or at meals. We need to learn to talk with God and think about God often during the day." She paused. "What else?"

"Well, I think if we didn't ever read the Bible, we'd starve to death as Christians," Angela said.

"Yes! *Bible reading!* Extremely important, and not just on Sundays but every day," Pastor David said as the children wrote "Bible reading" in their charts. "Let me make a suggestion to all of you. Since you've already read the book of Mark, go next to the book of Matthew, then Luke, then John. Then you can start back with Mark again until you become very familiar with the story of the life and ministry of Jesus, our Lord and Savior." He paused. "Anything else?"

CHAPTER 8

"What about *worship?*" Tyrel said, as he began writing the word in his nutrition chart.

"Thanks, Tyrel. Regular worship is extremely important. That's why we gather every week to worship. It keeps us on track. It nourishes and feeds our souls. But what about the other days of the week?"

Daniel said, "I've found that doing the daily assignments has really helped me grow in my faith. Reading the Bible and prayer seem to be the most important part."

"Good, Daniel, and I hope you'll continue to worship, not just on Sundays but every day, by reading the Bible and praying often. It will be important to discipline yourself and set aside a regular time to do it. When you do, you'll find that it feeds your soul. Can you think of anything else?"

"Let's not forget *service!*" Joy added, and the whole group wrote the word in the chart. "I think whenever I serve my family or friends, even when I'm friendly with someone who isn't very popular, it helps my faith grow. I think God wants us to love and serve each other. Don't you?"

"And let's not forget attending Sunday school and youth groups," Tyrel said.

"Okay, let's write in the word *attendance* to mean all of that," Pastor David said. "I guess we've all seen the benefit of being a part of this class, and the same is true for other groups in the church. I wouldn't want to miss being a part of the activities of the church. When we go, we grow."

"There's one more that I want to be sure to get on the chart," said Pastor Maria. "Write down the word giving! We could use the word *stewardship,* but that's kind of long. It means that we need to be generous with our talent, money, and time. When we give, we grow in our faith. Giving is good for the soul."

"I sometimes wonder how much I should give of my money to God," said Angela. "My parents tithe to the church. But how much should I give?"

"The word *tithe* comes from the Bible and means that we give 10 percent of all that comes to us back to God, who gave it all to us in the first place." Pastor Maria smiled. "Of all the money that comes to us, David and I do the math and give one tenth of it in the offering plate on Sunday."

"So if I make ten dollars mowing the lawn," Angela said, "God expects me to give back one dollar?"

"Right!" Pastor David said. "And our generosity and willingness to give to God are very good for our souls. Now there's one more word I can think of that I want to be sure is on our charts, and it's the word *witness!*"

The group wrote the word as Pastor David explained what he meant. "I find that whenever I am able to express my faith to others and tell them how much I respect and love Jesus, it helps me grow in my confidence and faith. I'd encourage each of you to tell your friends about the baptism coming up and invite them to come."

Pastor Maria said, "Now look at that large space at the bottom of the chart that starts with 'the most important thing is...' What do you think might be the most important part of growing in our Christian life?"

 discussion

The class discussed this question for a while, and there were many good ideas about what is most important. But then Pastor Maria suggested, "Write in these letters: W.W.J.D. They stand for 'What Would Jesus Do?' As you live your Christian life, always do what Jesus would want you to do. Evaluate all of your decisions, activities, goals, habits, friendships, dating relationships, what you watch on TV—everything based on what you think Jesus would want you to do. And I can guarantee you that you'll grow to be a mature and dynamic Christian disciple and follower of Jesus Christ."

Pastor David added, "I couldn't have said it better. Being a disciple of Jesus isn't just one small part of my life. Jesus is all of my life and affects every part of the way I live my life. In fact, that's what Paul writes to the Ephesians in our Bible reading for today. Let's turn to Ephesians 3:11–16 and read it together."

 activity   discussion

Esteban read the passage and the class discussed and filled in the blanks. They looked up the word *grow* in a dictionary, wrote the definition, and then discussed together what it meant for them to grow in their faith. After they set some goals for spiritual growth, they each wrote a prayer.

Scripture for Today: Read Ephesians 3:11–16

According to verse 16, how are we to grow up? _____

_____

_____

_____

_____

As a disciple, who do I need to believe is at the head or in charge of my life now? _____

_____

_____

_____

_____

If I am to live as a disciple of Jesus, I will need to _____

_____

_____

_____

_____

How does the body of Christ, the church, grow and become stronger? *(v. 16)* _____
_____
_____
_____

The Big Word: GROW

Dictionary definition: _____
_____
_____
_____

If I want to grow in Christ and faith, I will need to spend time _____
_____
_____
_____

Here are three goals for my own spiritual growth:

1. _____
2. _____
3. _____

My Prayer for Today

Thank you, God, that during this study you have helped me to understand that ____
_____
_____
_____

I pray that in the future you will always be there to help me _____
_____
_____
_____

I promise you that I will _____
_____
_____
_____

Thank you for _____

_____

_____

_____

Amen.

When they all had completed writing their prayers, Pastor David and Maria suggested a group hug. As they huddled together in Christian community, the body of Christ, Pastor Maria spoke these words in a prayer to God:

"Dear God, thank you for shaping us into a community of love. It is so good to be a part of your church and to share love with Angela, Esteban, Tyrel, Daniel, and Joy, new disciples of Jesus. We look forward to Easter and the baptism. In the days ahead, help us all to grow in our faith that we might be better able to love and serve you and the world you've called us to serve. In the name of Jesus Christ. Amen."

After the prayer, Pastor David said, "And now we want each of you to add your name to the list of those who have completed the *Bridges of Promise*. Let's log on to www.abc-usa.org and find the *Bridges of Promise* site."

 activity

As the children typed their names, they sensed that they were a part of something much bigger than their little class, bigger even than First Baptist Church, bigger even than the American Baptist Churches USA. They were a part of the followers of Jesus Christ all over the globe, members of the body of Christ. And now it was their turn and their time to live their lives, yes, even give themselves totally—heart, mind, body, and soul—for Jesus Christ. And they all knew in their hearts that they were looking forward not only to Easter day and baptism, but to a lifetime of growing in Christ.

Activity #1: Getting Acquainted

My full name is ...

_____ _____

I like to ...

◉ _____

◉ _____

◉ _____

◉ _____

◉ _____

My favorite pizza toppings ...

◉ _____

◉ _____

◉ _____

I'm here because ...

_____

_____

_____

_____

Activity #2: Mountain of Promise

1. Tear the sheet from the book.
2. Cut on the bold lines (not the dotted lines).
3. Fold on the dotted lines and attach with tape.
4. Label the four sides of the mountain: Body, Heart, Mind, Soul

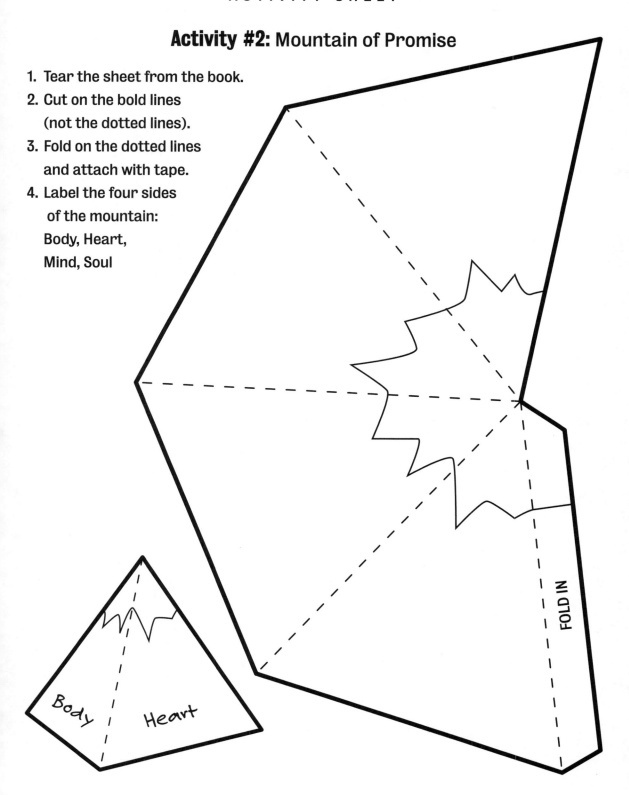

FOLD IN

Body | Heart

Activity #3 (side 1): The way I picture God

Directions: First think about God. Then in the picture frame below, use markers, pencils, or crayons to draw the way you picture God.

Turn this sheet over to continue the activity.

Activity #3 (side 2): The way I would describe God

Ancient manuscripts and scrolls described God and God's relationship to people. Try to be a "scribe" and de–scribe God in your own words.

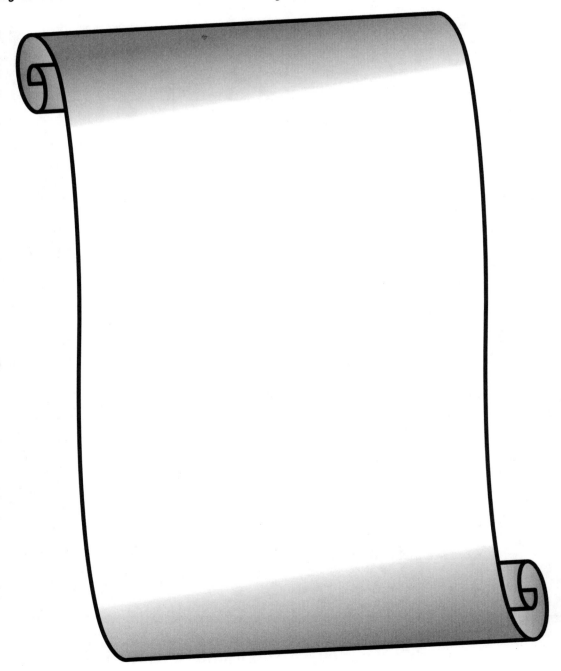

Activity #4: Steps on the Bridge to God

Directions:

1. Place two chairs back to back, approximately three feet apart from each other. Label one chair "God," and the second, "People." Connect the two chairs with a long strip of masking tape.
2. Cut out each of the bridge sections below. Attach each one to the masking-tape bridge as you read and discuss each Scripture.
3. Connect all the sections until they form a bridge from "God" to "People."

First Step:
Romans 3:22-23
Admit your sin!

Second Step:
Romans 6:23
Know the consequence for sin!

Third Step:
Romans 5:8-9
Know that you can be forgiven!

Fourth Step:
1 John 1:9
Confess your sins to God!

Fifth Step:
John 1:12
Choose to believe!

Sixth Step:
Romans 10:9-10
Have faith and say you believe!

Seventh Step:
Matthew 16:24-25
Give your whole life to follow Jesus!

Eighth Step:
Mark 12:28-31
Love God, love others, love yourself!

Activity #5 (side 1): What makes a church Baptist?

Below is a list of some Baptist beliefs and practices.
Read them carefully, and decide if they are true or false.

True   **False**

O   O   The New Testament is our guide
                       for Christian living.

O   O   Each person may come to God
                       directly through Jesus Christ.

O   O   Each person has a right to worship God
                       in his or her own way.

O   O   Only those who accept Jesus as their
                       Savior and Lord are to be baptized.

O   O   The way Baptists baptize is the way Jesus
                       was baptized—by going completely
                       underwater (immersion).

O   O   Each local church has the right to decide its
                       own business and ways of doing things without
                       a higher authority telling it what to do.

O   O   There are two ordinances (things we do that
                       Jesus told us to do): baptism and Communion,
                       also called the Lord's Supper.

O   O   The church and the government need to be
                       separate so that the government isn't telling
                       the church what to believe and how to worship.

O   O   It is good for individual churches to work
                       together with other churches. Jesus Christ
                       wants us to work together.

After you have discussed your answers on this page, turn the page over
and work together to fill in the blanks about your own church.

Activity #5 (side 2): Interesting things about

_____ Church

(Fill in the name of the church you attend.)

⊙ My church was organized in the year _____

⊙ The names of some of the people who started my church are

_____

⊙ The first pastor was _____

⊙ The church has met in _____ buildings

⊙ The present church building was built in the year _____

⊙ Our church's total budget for this year is around $ _____

⊙ Most of that money comes from _____

⊙ Of this amount of money, the church gives about $ _____
to mission projects outside the church

⊙ Our church has about _____ members

⊙ A person who wants to be a member of my church needs to

_____

_____

_____

_____

Activity #6: The Church

1. Remove the sheet from the book.
2. Cut on the bold lines (not the dotted lines).
3. Fold on the dotted lines and attach with tape.
4. Label the four sides of the mountain: Fellowship, Worship, Education, Mission

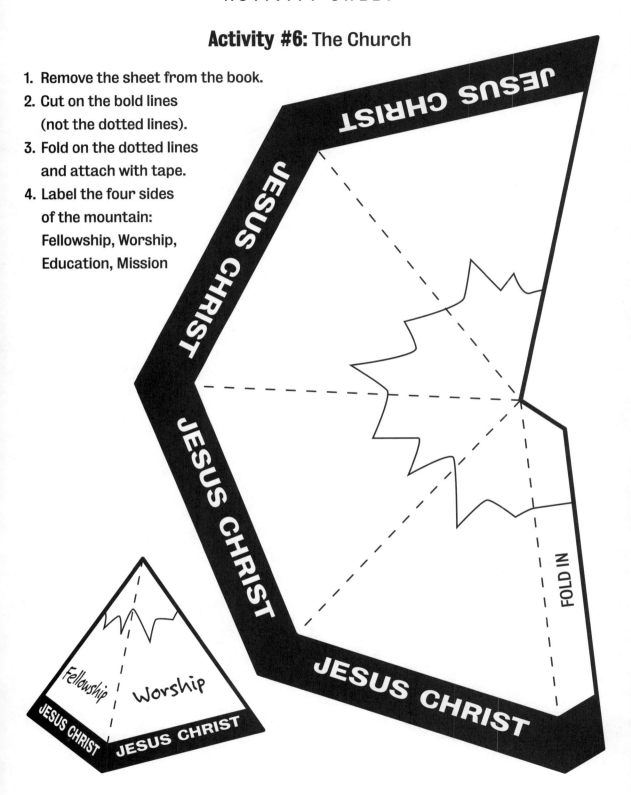

Activity #7: My Declaration of Promise to God

My Decisions

I believe that God has invited me to choose to follow Jesus as my Lord and Savior, my bridge to God, and to give my whole life—mind, body, heart, and soul—to God. Therefore, these are my decisions:

		Not	
Yes	No	Yet	
O	O	O	1. I believe Jesus Christ is God's Son, and I accept him as my Lord and Savior.
O	O	O	2. I will try to live as a true follower of Jesus Christ at all times and in all places.
O	O	O	3. I will think and pray about what it means to be a follower of Jesus Christ before deciding to be baptized and become a member of my church.
O	O	O	4. I have decided to be baptized.
O	O	O	5. I have decided that I want to become a member of my church.
O	O	O	6. Other decisions: _____

_____

_____

Signature: _____

Date: _____

Activity #8 (side 1): Bridges of Promise

Activity #8 (side 2): Bridges of Promise

One way I can be like a bridge in helping others...

at home:

at church:

at school:

in my neighborhood:

with the poor:

Activity #9: Good Nutrition

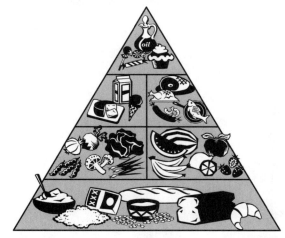

Nutrition for Physical Health
Feeding the Body

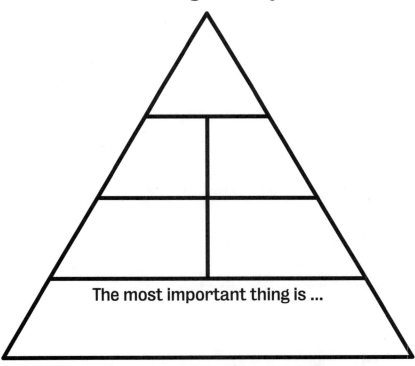

The most important thing is ...

Nutrition for Spiritual Health
Feeding the Soul

(Write in some of the things that help to keep us strong and healthy in our Christian faith.)